Diversity in Computer Science

Pernille Bjørn
Maria Menendez-Blanco • Valeria Borsotti

Diversity in Computer Science

Design Artefacts for Equity and Inclusion

 Springer

Pernille Bjørn
University of Copenhagen
Copenhagen, Denmark

Valeria Borsotti
University of Copenhagen
Copenhagen, Denmark

Maria Menendez-Blanco
Free University of Bozen-Bolzano
Bolzano, Italy

ISBN 978-3-031-13313-8   ISBN 978-3-031-13314-5   (eBook)
https://doi.org/10.1007/978-3-031-13314-5

This Springer imprint is published by the registered company Springer Nature Switzerland AG
The registered company address is: Gewerbestrasse 11, 6330 Cham, Switzerland

Introduction

Diversity in Computer Science: Design Artefacts for Equity and Inclusion presents and documents the principles, results, and learnings behind the research initiative FemTech.dk, which was created in 2016 and continues today as an important part of the Department of Computer Science at the University of Copenhagen's strategic development for years to come. However, this book is also the story of how we (the authors) as computer science researchers embarked on a journey to engage with a new research field – *equity and gender in computing* – about which we had only sporadic knowledge when we began. We refer here to equity and gender in computing as *a research field* – but in reality, this research field is *a multiplicity* of entangled paths, concepts, and directions that forms important and critical insights about society, gender, politics, and infrastructures which are published in different venues and often have very different sets of criteria, values, and assumptions. Thus, part of our journey is also to learn and engage with all these different streams of research, concepts, and theoretical approaches and, through these engagements, to identify and develop our own theoretical platform, which has a foundation in our research backgrounds in human computer interaction broadly – and interaction design and computer supported cooperative work specifically. We chose in this book to include insights about our own journey, including failures and successes we experienced along the way. In this way, we choose to become vulnerable through our writing and hope that readers will appreciate our efforts in making transparent and visible those aspects of research that sometimes remain invisible in research publications. Demonstrating vulnerability in research can be scary and present risks – however, in true equity and inclusion research, personal self-disclosure is a common practice (Hamidi et al. 2018; Keyes 2018) that allows peers to consider the perspectives through which research activities are being conducted and accomplished. Among the main theoretical assumptions within equity and inclusion research is that who you are and where you come from matter and shape the kinds of research endeavours you can accomplish (Muller 2011; Rode 2011; Spiel et al. 2020). Thus, when you study a phenomenon, you always take a position and study from 'somewhere' (Haraway 1990), and for peers to fully judge your work and contribution – and to consider how your work embraces the complexities of the contextual considerations – they need insights into your position. We hope readers of this book can learn from our mistakes and challenges and in this way push equity and inclusion research as well as interventions forward, changing the state of diversity in computer science.

How to Read This Book

This book is written with five different audiences in mind. Surely, you can decide to read the whole book from cover to cover. We have intentionally made the book short with many illustrations and expect that readers can get through it in appropriate time and hopefully enjoy all the content. However, if you have specific interests, knowledge, or insights you want to start with, we will here provide suggestions for directed reading.

One audience is computer science teachers (at all levels but mostly high school and up) who are interested in thinking about diversity and equity when designing their classrooms, their assignments, and interactions. While our book is not about new teaching methods or computer science curriculum per se, the FemTech principles demonstrated through the design artefacts Cyberbear, Cryptosphere, and GRACE can inform teachers on how to think differently about their curriculum and teaching environments. We expect that such readers would benefit from focusing their reading on Chaps. 4, 5, and 6. It is in these chapters that we introduce the FemTech design principles and our design artefacts, and present the data and results from our workshops and interventions.

A second audience includes the decision-makers, managers, and policymakers who lead tech organizations or computer science departments and want to have dedicated strategies for diversity, equity, and inclusion initiatives beyond 'window dressing'. For these readers we suggest focusing their readings on Chaps. 7, 8, and 9. Of specific interest for management at universities (and computer science departments), we would include reading Chap. 1.

A third audience includes researchers who do research within equity in computing within areas such as software development, human computer interaction, computer supported cooperative work, and design research. For these readers we would suggest reading Chaps. 2, 3, 4, 5, and 6. These chapters introduce our research, methods, and findings.

A fourth audience includes tech organizations and unions, who are in the unique position of being able to make a concrete impact and push for equity within the computing industry. For this audience, we suggest reading Chaps. 7, 8, and 9 – to find a way to move organizations from only celebrating International Women's Day on March 8 each year to making real change.

The fifth audience includes journalists, the public, and other individuals who have an interest in questions such as: Why are there so few women in computing and tech organizations in Denmark? What are the historic reasons for computer science departments to have so few women? What can we do about it?

There might be even more audiences who have an interest in this book – we hope so – and therefore we have been dedicated to making the book as available as possible for a large audience in both Denmark and internationally. To help all audiences navigate the book, we next introduce each chapter briefly. Further, there are lists of all tables and figures.

The book contains nine chapters of different lengths and foci. 'Introduction' sets the stage for the book through the introduction you are currently reading. We suggest that all readers use this chapter and the table of contents to navigate the book for directed reading.

Chapter 1, 'The State of Diversity in Computer Science in 2022', focuses on the state of diversity in computer science in 2022 in Denmark. The chapter includes historic facts about three women pioneers in computing – and introduces gender statistics about PhD degrees and PhD supervision in the Department of Computer Science at the University of Copenhagen. We suggest that you read this chapter if you are interested in the history of computer science in Denmark and are puzzled about why we know so little about the women.

Chapter 2, 'Femtech.dk Research Initiative', introduces FemTech.dk, the research interest, our aim, and contextual situations, which is the foundation for the book. If you are considering being inspired by the FemTech work, it is important to understand the basic interests and assumptions behind the approach, and thus we suggest reading this chapter.

Chapter 3, 'Interventionist Research', introduces the research method used in FemTech. Chapter 3 includes reflections on how our work is situated within the Scandinavian approach to participatory design and action research. Finally, the chapter introduces our interventionist agenda and provides reflections on our role as researchers. This chapter will be most interesting for readers who want to know about the epistemological assumptions behind our work.

Chapter 4, 'Makerspace Methodologies & Design Principles', situates our work in the physical DIY (do-it-yourself) computing laboratory and explicates how moving the narrative on computer science from desktop research to the lab is a dedicated interest and concern of our work. Further, the chapter includes how we mobilized various resources in our attempt to create and build physical places for our work. The chapter also introduces the four FemTech design principles, on which all our artefacts and interventions have been based.

Chapter 5, 'Cyberbear & Cryptosphere: Sociomaterial-Design, Social Belonging, and Gender Representations', is one of the core chapters in the book. The chapter presents the research we did considering the design of FemTech artefacts and the events we organized for women who do not see themselves as belonging to computing. If you are organizing events or other activities – or considering concrete new outreach strategies for your diversity work – we suggest reading this chapter.

Chapter 6, 'GRACE: Designing Sociomaterial Assemblages Unpacking Gender Equity in Computing', is the second core chapter in this book. The chapter focuses on the FemTech artefact GRACE, an installation for discussing and reflecting on gender in computing. The chapter includes all the research results we gained using GRACE as an artefact of inquiry. If you are interested in provocative design artefacts and how they can travel and be used for engaging people in conversations, you should read this chapter.

Chapter 7, 'Equity & Inclusion', is a reflective chapter which introduces important vocabulary for organizations and individuals to consider when thinking about equity, diversity, and inclusion. The chapter is core reading if you are involved in any kind of diversity work in your organization – in particular, we suggest that all decision-makers in tech organizations as well as computer science university departments read this chapter.

Chapter 8, 'Organizational Change for Equity and Inclusion', introduces three propositions, based on all our work, which can help move 'diversity, equity, and inclusion' work in organizations. We suggest that decision-makers and managers at all levels involved in tech organizations or computer science departments read this chapter. Also, unions, union representatives, and political policymakers would benefit from reading this chapter, in their attempt to move the agenda forward in a concrete manner.

Finally, in Chap. 9, 'Final Reflections', we reflect on our own learnings, which we hope will benefit others as they move the agenda forward. This includes normative statements about what kind of activities and initiatives we found to be beneficial if tech organizations and computer science departments truly are to reach equal gender representation within computer science and technology development.

Acknowledgements

FemTech.dk could not have existed if not for the many people, students, colleagues, and participants who engaged with and helped us develop concepts, organize events, design artefacts, and provide a supportive and enjoyable work environment. Martin Dybdal needs special thanks for taking on the FemTech workshop after us, joining our efforts with the UCPH Makerspace, and continuing to develop the concept as well as developing and executing the kick-starter course mainstreaming our efforts. We thank Naja Holten Møller, Stina Matthiesen, Karim Jabbar, Arni Mar Einarsson, and Nelson Tenorio for joining us in developing and executing the MakerWeeks and for being amazing and supportive colleagues always ready to test our prototypes and provide reflective feedback. Further, we must thank Naja Holten Møller, Stina Mathiasen, Mia Meldgaard Jensen, and Kasper Lorentzen, who joined as teachers for the FemTech workshop in 2017. We thank Paul Strohmeier for allowing us to use his e-textile research as part of the Cyberbear workshop in 2017 and Christoffer Belange, who was instrumental in the implementation of the Cryptosphere for the workshop in 2018. We also thank all the computer science students who joined our activities – especially the co-teachers for the FemTech workshop in 2018, Rasmus Hvid Schmidt and Maja Hvidtfeldt Håkansson. Maja Hvidtfeld Håkansson also continued on for additional FemTech workshops, for the kick-starter course, and made amazing architectural drawings for our dream makerspace design. Thank to Haakon Lund and Trine Louise Schreiber for inviting us to join the special issue on 'makerspaces, makers, and make movement' in 2018, and Mette Seistrup for supporting us with room and equipment at KUA3 when we needed it. We also thank Claus Witfelt, who has been very supportive in sending his students to join the FemTech workshops each year. We also thank all the participants who have joined the FemTech workshops over the years.

Huge thanks go to Stine Broen Christensen, from Underbroen, who invited us to present GRACE at Copenhagen Makers in 2017 in Carlsbergbyen; Hans Dybkjær, for developing the origami design for the GRACE installation; Peter Bjørn Rasmussen and Lise Dandanel, for composing and performing the music for the GRACE events; Jesper Bruun, for collecting data about GRACE during Copenhagen Makers; and Kasper Lorentzen, for implementing the GRACE app. Also, thanks to

Chi Pham, who joined the Copenhagen Maker event in 2017. We would also like to mention Stavris Solo, who as the lab manager at the Southern campus has always supported our efforts for the MakerWeek and all kinds of other events – and for providing a home for the GRACE installation.

We also thank all the students who have joined the Makerspace or supported the FemTech research in different ways by joining workshops, by doing their master's thesis as part of FemTech, or by supporting the effort and being amazing students. In particular, we would like to mention Christoffer Belange, Mette Hermansen, Jenny Margrethe Vej, Søren Sørensen, Jonathan Jensen, Olivia Linder Tabel, and Frederik Freiesleben, who each have produced excellent research within FemTech as part of their master's or bachelor's thesis.

We thank Heike Vögele, for visiting us in Copenhagen and collecting data about makerspaces; Sine Zambach, for featuring FemTech in her book; Lone Kofoed, for featuring GRACE in Wilful Technologies; and Ben Christensen, for inviting us to talk about FemTech at SAP, #sheinnovate in New York. We thank Martha Larson and Susanne Boll for inviting us to present the keynote at ACM MM 2019 in Nice, France.

Finally, we also thank the former head of department, Mads Nielsen, for supporting the FemTech initiatives from the beginning – and the current head of department, Jakob Grue Simonsen, for continuing to support FemTech as well as prioritizing the agenda of Inclusive DIKU.

FemTech continues today as an important research-based initiative in the Department of Computer Science, University of Copenhagen, especially with the research of the third author, Valeria Borsotti, PhD, and her role as diversity chair in the department. As a result, two new initiatives were created in 2021: Code of Conduct and Inclusive DIKU. Creating organizational transformation requires persistence, commitment, time, effort, resources, and collaborative engagement.

Contents

List of Figures

List of Tables

About the Authors

Pernille Bjørn, PhD, is an internationally recognized and highly esteemed researcher within the computer science area human computer interaction (HCI), with a specialized focus on computer supported cooperative work (CSCW). Her research includes the design of information technologies supporting healthcare professionals in hospitals (e.g., in emergency departments), communication technologies supporting distributed collaboration (e.g., global software development), and the role of information infrastructures in tech entrepreneurship (e.g., the role of blockchain technology or entrepreneurship under occupation). Most recently her research interest is focused on the potential of cooperative virtual reality supporting architectural design of hospitals and safety training in the maritime domain, and on how to re-think and design technologies creating the future of work after the pandemic.

Dr. Bjørn's core research interest is the exploration and design of innovative technologies which support human interaction, utilizing and challenging the potentials of digital visions by combining analogue and digital materials (e.g., utilizing IoT technologies [Internet-of-Things]). Her work has been published in the most prestigious journals within her field, including the *Journal of Computer Supported Cooperative Work*, *Human Computer Interaction*, and *Information System Journal*, and presented at prestigious conferences including the European Conference in Computer Supported Cooperative Work (ECSCW), the ACM Conference on Computer Supported Cooperative Work (CSCW), and the ACM CHI Conference on Human Factors in Computer Systems. Further, Dr. Bjørn has been invited to deliver keynotes at large conferences including ICGSE/GSE in Montreal, Canada, and ACM Multimedia in Nice, France. Professor Bjørn has served in many trusted academic service roles within her field, including as Papers Co-chair for the CHI conference in 2020 and 2021, as Papers Co-chair for the ACM CSCW conference in 2016, and as Papers Co-chair for the ECSCW in 2018.

Professor Bjørn has an international profile and has conducted research outside Denmark for more than 4 years, including as a guest professor at the University of Washington, Seattle, in the Department of Human Centered Design & Engineering (2018–2019); a guest researcher at the University of California, Irvine, in the

Department of Informatics (2013–2014); as a guest researcher at the Indian Institute of Management, Bangalore, India (several shorter stays between 2010 and 2014); and as a postdoctoral fellow at Simon Fraser University, Vancouver, Canada, in the Department of Communication (2006–2008).

Dr. Bjørn became the first woman to become full professor in the Department of Computer Science at the University of Copenhagen (DIKU), when she was recruited in 2015. Prior to her position at DIKU, she was associate professor (and shortly tenure-track assistant professor) at the IT University of Copenhagen. She earned her PhD in computer science from Roskilde University in 2007, which she defended in December 2006. Since 2019, Professor Bjørn has served as deputy head of department for research in the Department of Computer Science, University of Copenhagen.

Professor Bjørn created FemTech.dk in 2016, together with Dr. Maria Menendez-Blanco, and continues the work currently with PhD candidate Valeria Borsotti. Further, she created AtariWomen.org in 2018–2019 together with Dr. Daniela Rosner as part of her Fulbright scholarship, which documents the contributions of women and other gender minorities in the early days of computer game development in the USA through design artefacts. She is proud that AtariWomen artefacts have been displayed at museums in Seattle and, most recently, at the Danish National Gallery in relation to International Women's Day in March 2022.

Maria Menendez-Blanco, PhD, is an interaction design researcher working in the fields of human computer interaction, computer supported collaborative work, and participatory design. Her research focuses on how digital technologies can enable, or hinder, democratic processes of participation. She follows an action research approach to the design of digital platforms, interactive artefacts, and public events that represent complex societal concerns (e.g., inclusion, discrimination, harassment). In her work, she often collaborates with collectives, practitioners, and the public administration. Topics related to gender and intersectional aspects are core to her research – and to her academic and personal life. Following-up on her work in FemTech.dk, she is working on how interactive data representations can foster debates on gender.

Dr. Menendez-Blanco's work has been published in top-tier journals in her field including the *Journal of Computer Supported Cooperative Work*, *Human–Computer Interaction*, and the *Interactional Journal of Human Computer Studies*. She has been invited to deliver keynotes at the ACM Multimedia conference in Nice, France. She regularly serves as chair in the most prestigious conferences in her fields such as the ACM Conference on Human Factors in Computing Systems. Her work has received several awards and personal grants from international institutions such as the ACM Special Interest Group on Computer Human Interaction and the European Institute of Technology (EIT Digital).

Dr. Menendez-Blanco has an international profile and has conducted research in the Netherlands, Italy, Spain, and Denmark for the last 15 years. Currently she works an assistant professor in the Computer Science Faculty at the Free University of Bozen-Bolzano, Italy. She holds a PhD in information and communication technology from the Department of Information Engineering and Computer Science at the University of Trento, Italy, and in innovation and entrepreneurship from EIT

Digital. She obtained a professional doctorate in engineering in user-system interaction from the Technical University of Eindhoven, the Netherlands.

Valeria Borsotti is a digital anthropologist and PhD candidate in the Department of Computer Science at the University of Copenhagen (Denmark), where she also serves as diversity chair. She holds an MS in anthropology and a BA in literary theory. Her research focuses on equity, accessibility, and inclusivity in computing education, in particular looking at how social norms and values around gender and dis/ability are embedded in humour, spaces, artefacts, and organizational practices – and how we can effect positive change as a collective. Her research mixes ethnography, autoethnography, play, and design, and her work has been published and presented in high profile journals and conferences such as the *Journal of Computer Supported Cooperative Work* (JCSCW) and the International Conference on Software Engineering (ICSE), where her previous qualitative study on the gender barriers in Danish software development education has received a best paper award. Her previous work at the intersection of anthropology and literary theory, examining how poetry challenges and subverts racist narratives in Denmark, has been featured in an anthology published by the Firenze University Press.

Valeria Borsotti's research is part of the FemTech.dk program led by Professor Pernille Bjørn at the University of Copenhagen. Before her PhD, Valeria gained several years of experience in Italy, Sweden, the USA, and Denmark, working with projects related to furthering social inclusion in art museums and cultural institutions, educational institutions, and non-profits.

Chapter 1
The State of Diversity in Computer Science in 2022

'Datalogy' (or computer science) is the academic foundation and practice that determines how digital technologies are designed, developed, and introduced into peoples' lives. Digital technologies shape society, life, and work and influence how people think and act with technology in all aspects of life. In a democracy it is vital that the people who create technology mirror the society's diversity, to ensure that new digital technologies do not constrain people's agency but enable people to act and take part in society. Today, in 2022, diversity and inclusion is one of the main challenges for computer science as a field and profession in Western countries such as Denmark and the USA (Frieze and Quesenberry 2019; Borsotti and Bjørn 2022), and studies have shown that computer science will not reach gender parity in this century (Holman et al. 2018) without interventions directed at change.

Three Pioneer Women in Computer Science in Denmark

All the research we present in this book took place in the Department of Computer Science at the University of Copenhagen (Datalogisk Institut Københavns Universitet [DIKU]), in Denmark. Thus, our work is situated in Denmark, and since gender is culturally shaped (Butler 1999), providing some contextual information about the Computer Science Department is important. The University of Copenhagen was established in 1479 and is the oldest university in Denmark and the second oldest in Scandinavia (Uppsala University in Sweden was established in 1477). DIKU was established in 1970 by Turing Award winner Peter Naur and grew out of the Department of Mathematics. DIKU was thus created during the '68 student rebellion at universities in Denmark, where students and administrative personnel fought for voice and decision power in the universities, thus challenging the prior unified power owned only by professors (Hansen 1997). At this time, universities in Denmark transformed from elite institutions for the few to mass universities that were democratically organized. At DIKU this meant that students were highly

© The Author(s) 2023
P. Bjørn et al., *Diversity in Computer Science*,
https://doi.org/10.1007/978-3-031-13314-5_1

engaged with the department's planning and teaching – active in creating the institution – and that Head of Department was an elected position. At that time approximately 20% of the students were women (Sveinsdottir and Frøkjær 1988), and one of the core faculty members creating the department in 1970 was professor Edda Sveindottir (1936–2022). Considered the first woman computer scientist in Denmark, Professor Sveindottir was the first woman to be appointed Head of Department for Computer Science. Professor Sveindottir was never appointed full professor at DIKU, remaining an associate professor until she left DIKU, but became a full professor at Roskilde University, where she stayed until her retirement. Professor Sveindottir is to date the only woman Head of Department at DIKU, and her pioneering research and impact on the development of computer science in Denmark is well celebrated.

The PhD degree was introduced in Denmark in 1987, and the first woman to earn the degree in computer science in Denmark was at Aarhus University, the second largest university in Denmark, Professor Susanne Bødker, that same year. The Department of Computer Science at Aarhus University was established in 1975 – and Professor Bødker continues to be one of Denmark's most influential and international leading computer science researchers to this day. The first woman to earn a PhD in computer science at DIKU was Professor Emeritus Elin Rønby Pedersen, in 1988. After finishing her PhD with Peter Naur as supervisor, Professor Pedersen become associate professor at Roskilde University. She left Denmark and academia and moved on to industry at Google and Microsoft for more than 25 years. Professor Rønby Pedersen returned to Denmark in 2021, continuing as a senior research scientist at Google, but was also appointed professor at the University of Southern Denmark.

There is no doubt that these amazing women all had – and still have – a huge impact on how computer science research has developed in Denmark and internationally. They have each in different ways been pioneers and trailblazers! Unfortunately, they are also only a very small set of the very few women who managed to succeed in computer science academia in Denmark during the period 1970–2010. Let's look at the numbers. First, however, it is important to mention that we are aware that gender is not a binary construct divided into only two categories: women and men. However, for reporting numbers we are basing our observations on the available historical data, which are reported in binary terms.

Lack of Diversity: PhD Degrees & PhD Supervisors

The PhD degree is the highest obtainable academic degree, and it documents a person's research skills and qualifications. Since its introduction to Danish academia in 1987 (there were other merit systems in Denmark before that), the PhD degree has been a requirement for obtaining a faculty position at universities in Denmark and internationally. Thus, to understand the diversity potentials in universities, one must start by looking at the numbers for people obtaining the PhD degree.

If we look at the numbers from the Department of Computer Science at University of Copenhagen (DIKU) focusing on PhD degrees, we find the following. Since the PhD degree was introduced in 1987 in Denmark, only 23 women have been awarded the degree in computer science from DIKU, whereas 155 men have been awarded the degree. Of the 35 years that DIKU have been awarding PhD degrees, there have been 21 years with no women graduating with a PhD degree but only 2 years for men. In the period 1987–1997, only 4 women received the PhD degree in computer science from DIKU, whereas 37 men did; and in the period 1998–2008, only 2 women received the PhD degree from DIKU, whereas 38 men did. If we look at the statistics for the last 5 years (2017–2021), 8 women and 42 men graduated with a PhD degree from DIKU. While PhD degrees have been awarded to women from DIKU since 1988, the numbers are clearly unbalanced (Table 1.1).

The Privilege of PhD Supervision

To fully comprehend the gender unbalance in the Computer Science faculty at DIKU, it is important to consider the different measures and metrics by which faculty success is considered. While there has been a change in recent decades in terms of evaluating the impact and research quality of universities in Denmark – with an increased focus on citation indexes, grant procurements, and relevance to industry – most academics would agree that PhD education continues to be an important measure both nationally and internationally within computer science. Supervising and graduating PhD students is thus a privilege that allows faculty to extend their research agenda and continue their personal research interests. Having the opportunity to supervise PhD students in Denmark depends on individuals' success in winning research grants to pay for those students. However, as clearly demonstrated by research on grant distributions in Denmark (Aagaard et al. 2018; Madsen and Aagaard 2020), the 20% most-grant-winning researchers in Denmark are awarded 75% of all available funds (Norn 2019). Further, even considering the gender unbalance in the overall Danish academic environment across all topic areas, only 22% of all funds are allocated to female PIs.

> Overall, 40% of Danish researchers are female, while this is the case for only 34% of the grantees. However, when considering the distribution of grants and funding amounts only 29% of all grants have a female PI, and only 22% of all funding is allocated to a female PI. (Madsen and Aagaard 2020)

Funding influences career advancement in academia, not only in terms of having available resources to do research but also as part of the merit that provides access to faculty positions. The ability to win funds is perceived as part of the qualification criteria for academic hiring – *and for the next funding application*. This means that researchers who have already demonstrated their ability in attracting funds are more likely to continue attracting new funds (safe bet). This phenomenon that scientists who have previously been successful are more likely to succeed again, producing

Table 1.1 PhD degree awarded in the period 1987–2021 from Department of Computer Science, University of Copenhagen

	Women	Men	All
2021	3	13	16
2020		8	8
2019	2	5	7
2018	2	9	11
2017	1	7	8
2016		8	8
2015			0
2014	3	3	6
2013	1	2	3
2012		7	7
2011	2	5	7
2010	3	7	10
2009		5	5
2008	1	10	11
2007	1	1	2
2006		4	4
2005		4	4
2004		2	2
2003		3	3
2002		4	4
2001		1	1
2000		2	2
1999		3	3
1998		4	4
1997		2	2
1996		5	5
1995		5	5
1994		6	6
1993	1	2	3
1992			0
1991	1	6	7
1990		3	3
1989	1	3	4
1988	1	4	5
1987		2	2
Total	23	155	178

increasing distinction, is referred to as the Matthaeus (or Matthew) effect (Bagilhole and Goode 2001). The Matthaeus affect refers to the Bible quote "For everyone who has will be given more, and he will have an abundance. But the one who does not have, even what he has will be taken away from him" (Matt. 25:29); the term was coined by sociologists Harriet Zuckerman and Robert K. Merton (Zuckerman and

Merton 1971), who studied the scientific elite of Nobel laureates in the USA (Merton 1968; Zuckerman 1977). Their research showed that in the matter of academic credit, credit is given to already famous people, and in cases of co-authorship where the authors have unequal reputations, the person who is best known gets more credit and the names of the additional authors tend to be forgotten (Merton 1968). If we apply this pattern of recognition and academic credit to the funding landscape in Denmark, the Matthaeus effect seems to apply given that only 20% of Danish researchers receive 75% of the complete available funding.

Access to external funding is highly connected to the privilege of PhD supervision in Denmark. First, in Denmark, PhD students are *both* students and employees, which means that they are accepted to the PhD school as a student but that their supervisor must be able to fund their salary as hired employees. Because of the decrease in universities spending basic funds on PhD students and a higher reliance on external funding for PhD employment, gaining the privilege to supervise PhD students relies heavily on individual faculty success in winning external funding to pay for PhD employment. Successful supervision of PhD students will in most cases lead to an increase in high-ranking publications, which in turn will increase the citation index of the individual PhD student as well as the supervisor – which again would improve the chances of winning research grants, and so forth. The increased pressure on securing grants and decreased chance of receiving funds mean that brilliant ideas and excellent qualifications are not enough to win. Innovative international initiatives try to reduce bias and improve openness to radical, non-mainstream ideas by implementing new mechanisms for distributing grants based on a lottery (Adam 2019), and Danish researchers have also suggested that the Danish funding landscape should consider such approaches (Baggersgaard 2021). In 2022, the Novo Nordisk Foundation, one of the largest private funders in Denmark, declared that they will experiment with partial randomization of fund distribution (Frandsen 2022).

Gender Distribution of PhD Supervisors

Given the unbalanced funding distribution, the low number of women PhD graduates, and the low number of women faculty in the Computer Science Department – we decided to explore the gender distribution of PhD *supervisors*. Associate and full professors can be PhD supervisors, and tenure-track assistant professors can be co-supervisors until they are promoted to associate professor. Examining the relationships between supervisors and their PhD students who graduated from DIKU during the period 1987–2021, we find no PhD student graduate with a woman supervisor until 2010. This means that for the *first 23 years* of DIKU awarding the PhD degree, *only men* received the privilege of supervising PhD students. There are multiple cases from the period 1990–2010 where the privilege and work of supervising a PhD student was shared by a group of supervisors. However, not until 2010 did a mixed-gender supervisory team graduate a PhD student. Even after 2010, women supervisors were a rarity – and of the 35 years (1987–2021) in which DIKU awarded the PhD degree, there were *31 years where no women* had the privilege of solo supervising PhD student graduating. In comparison, there is *only one year* without male supervisors, 1992, when no PhD student graduated from DIKU.

Of the 35 years, DIKU awarded the PhD degree to students with mixed-gender group supervisors in only 8 years, during the period 2010–2021. Further, in only 4 years were PhD graduates solo supervised by a woman (2010, 2019–2021), graduating in total 6 PhD students. There have been no women-only group supervisions and only 13 mixed-gender group supervisions in total over the 35 years, whereas there have been 27 men-only group supervisions. Co-supervision is also a privilege, which means that where a faculty member benefits from being a co-supervisor, it is most likely a man. In comparison, 133 PhD graduates from DIKU in all 35 years have been supervised by male supervisors. Graduating PhD students as a supervisor confers privilege and power, as it is a core measure for promotion. Further, extremely few PhD students experience women supervisors (Table 1.2).

Finally, we should mention that besides Professor Edda Sveinsdottir who was associate professor at DIKU until she left (1970–1987) and was promoted to full professor at Roskilde University; Senior Scientist Dr. Julia Lawall was also associate professor at DIKU during the period 2000–2011, before she left to work at INRIA. Both Edda Sveinsdottir and Julia Lawall were the solo women faculty during their time at DIKU. We have not been able to identify any women who were faculty at DIKU during the period 1987–2000. Corinna Cortes is VP at Google Research in New York, and also hold the title as adjunct professor at DIKU since 2011. Marleen de Bruijne was recruited as associate professor at DIKU in 2011; Christina Lioma was recruited as tenure-track assistant professor in 2012; and Aasa Feragan was recruited as associate professor in 2014; Katarzyna (Kate) Wac was recruited as associate professor in 2015; and Pernille Bjørn was recruited as full professor in 2015.

The point here is that to fully comprehend the state of affairs shaping the unbalanced gender representation in computer science in Denmark in general and at DIKU specifically, it is not enough to pay attention to the gender disparity between bachelor's and master's degree students; we must also look at the gender disparity within the PhD student cohorts – as well as the gender disparity within the faculty having the privilege of supervising PhD students.

Slow Change 2015–2022

In May 2015, DIKU hired a woman into a full professor position for the first time. As of 2022, DIKU has increased the number of women faculty for tenure-track assistant professors, associate professors, and full professors. For women faculty, DIKU has as of January 2022 *four full* professors (Professor Pernille Bjørn, recruited in 2015; Professor Marleen de Bruijne, promoted in 2018; Professor Christina Lioma, promoted in 2019; Professor Irina Shklovski, recruited in 2020), *three associate* professors (Associate Professor Melanie Ganz-Benjaminsen, promoted in

Table 1.2 Supervisors of PhD graduates, 1987–2021: 133 solo men supervision, 6 solo women supervision, 13 mixed-group supervision, 26 group of men supervisions, and 0 women group supervisions, for a total 178 PhD graduates

PhD *supervisors* 1987–2021				
Year	Man (solo)	Woman (solo)	Group supervision mixed gender	Group supervision men ONLY
1987	2			
1988	5			
1989	4			
1990	2			1
1991	7			
1992				
1993	3			
1994	6			
1995	5			
1996	5			
1997	2			
1998	3			1
1999	2			
2000	2			1
2001	1			
2002	3			1
2003	3			
2004	2			
2005	4			
2006	3			1
2007	2			
2008	11			
2009	5			
2010	6	**3**	1	
2011	7			
2012	7			
2013	1			2
2014	3		1	2
2015				
2016	3		2	3
2017	2		2	4
2018	5		1	5
2019	3	**1**	2	1
2020	3	**1**	1	3
2021	11	**1**	3	1

2021; Associate Professor Joanna Bergström, promoted in 2021; and Associate Professor Isabelle Augenstein, promoted in 2020), and *six assistant* professors (Tenure-Track Assistant Professor Maria Maistro, Tenure-Track Assistant Professor Sarah Homewood, Tenure-Track Assistant Professor Valkyrie Savage, Tenure-Track

Assistant Professor Naja Holten Møller, Tenure-Track Assistant Professor Hasti Seifi, and Assistant Professor Stina Matthiesen).

As of the beginning of 2022, DIKU has 13 women faculty, the majority recruited after 2017. We do not have the number of current PhD students with women supervisors; however, to the best of our knowledge, most of the women faculty are currently supervising PhD students, and in all tenure-track packages new faculty receive funding for one-half a PhD grant to help them begin their research. Further, women faculty have been included in department management since 2018 as Head of Section and since 2019 as Deputy Head of Department for research.

For historic documentation, it should be mentioned that Professor Aasa Feragen at the Danish Technical University (DTU) was recruited from her associate professor position at DIKU to become full professor at DTU in 2019; and that Professor Katarzyna (Kate) Wac was promoted to full professor at DIKU, but was immediately recruited by University of Geneva, Switzerland, in 2020. Finally, late Dr. Luana Micallef was assistant professor at DIKU 2018–2019.

The latest official statistics from the university as of September 2021 show that the current faculty (assistant, associate, and full professors) measured in full time positions is 85% men and 15% women (67 full time positions); while the numbers for PhD candidates are 65% men and 34% women (72 full time positions). At the Professor level the difference is 93% men and 7% women full professors.

The FemTech.dk initiative was started in 2016 with a focus on gender diversity within the bachelor's and master's student cohorts; however, the above numbers for the department provide important context for understanding the lack of gender diversity which has existed for many years. Improving gender diversity at universities cannot focus on bachelor's and master's students alone. We must include critical examination of gender diversity for PhD students and the representation of gender diversity in faculty. For excellent young students to engage with computer science, universities will benefit from demonstrating how people from different backgrounds can become successful within the field and profession. The 17 women faculty who have been or currently are at DIKU are such a small percentage of the full faculty who have been doing research and research-based teaching in the 52 years the department has existed (1970–2022).

Chapter 2
FemTech.dk Research Initiative

FemTech.dk is situated in the Department of Computer Science at University of Copenhagen Denmark and has been an ongoing inquiry into the specific circumstances within computer science that produce gender imbalance and includes activities dedicated to making a change through design interventions.

FemTech's Initial Focus on Bachelor's and Master's Students

FemTech.dk was created in 2016 to engage with research within gender and diversity and to explore the role of gender equity as part of digital technology design and development. FemTech.dk considers how and why computer science as a field and profession in Denmark has such a distinct unbalanced gender representation in the twenty-first century. The focus was initially on the student base of the bachelor's program in computer science, which from the 1980s until 2016 was remarkably smaller than for other science programs at the University of Copenhagen (Table 2.1).

In terms of numbers, *only* 15 women students entered the bachelor's degree program in 2012 and 2013, and *only* 12 women students entered the program in 2014. In each of these 3 years, more than 160 students entered the program in total. Reviewing the 15-year period 2000–2014, the share of women students in the program was 7% to 9%, the lowest percentage of women in a study program across all of the University of Copenhagen. To compare, in 2016 the share of women students in the Math program was 30%, and in Physics was 25%. Further, these percentages match those at other universities in Denmark.

Why do so few women choose to pursue a computer science degree in Denmark? More puzzling is that Denmark is known to score high on the gender-equality scale for the UN Sustainable Development Goals (SDG) (DataHub 2019), and that in Denmark all (theoretically) have equal access to free education. Danish university students do not pay tuition fees and receive economic support for living costs while enrolled in education from the government. Moreover, Denmark has paid parental

© The Author(s) 2023
P. Bjørn et al., *Diversity in Computer Science*,
https://doi.org/10.1007/978-3-031-13314-5_2

Table 2.1 University of Copenhagen, Educational services for data and systems

Percentage of Women in BSc and Msc (DIKU) vs. Year

Year	Percentage of Women
2000	9.50%
2001	9.52%
2002	8.81%
2003	8.29%
2004	8.21%
2005	7.91%
2006	8.08%
2007	7.27%
2008	7.38%
2009	7.06%
2010	7.26%
2011	7.34%
2012	8.87%
2013	8.91%
2014	8.41%

leave (also for students) and a childcare infrastructure that allows students to return to their studies or to work as parents. All these factors would otherwise be considered obstacles to attending university and choosing a well-paid career in technology development. Also, across all university programs, women students represent more than 50% of the student population. Still, there is a huge discrepancy between the availability of and access to pursue a degree in computer science and the number of women who choose to apply.

FemTech.dk Is About Research, Not Recruiting

While these numbers describe an important context for the FemTech.dk research initiative, we acknowledge that a sole focus on "numbers" risks addressing the gender imbalance as a communication or marketing concern, which will limit the research results and long-term impact. FemTech.dk *does not* have a communication and marketing agenda. Instead, it is a research initiative, where we treat our concerns about a *real-life phenomenon as a research concern*. Our research concern takes its starting point in experienced practice, but the fundamental research interest guiding our work is to *explore and unpack* the situated *fundamental assumptions, values, norms, and background knowledge* that serve as *the infrastructural socio-technical foundation* shaping the current contextual situations of gender imbalance.

As computer science researchers, we draw on technology design research methods – specifically what we label makerspace methodologies. Briefly, makerspace methodologies combines analog and digital means to design, create, and implement interventionist critical design artefacts as a vehicle for change. Our primary aim is not to attract women to computer science but to figure out how we can open computer science to allow people from different backgrounds and with different interests to engage with computer science as a field and profession where they can succeed. We do not want to change women to make them fit in; instead, we want to change the field to make it more inclusive. As Shaowen Bardzell and Jeffrey Bardzell so elegantly phrase it:

> if we want more women in computing, the feminist approach would suggest that rather than transforming women in primary and secondary education to better prepare them for undergraduate CS, we might also consider transforming undergraduate CS so that it more clearly relates to undergraduate women's own intellectual agendas. (Bardzell and Bardzell 2011, p. 679)

Inspired by feminist Human–Computer Interaction (Bardzell 2010; Rode 2011), the FemTech.dk research foundation is intended to extend the field of computer science and promote agendas that allow women (and other under-represented groups) to pursue their own agendas within the field. In all activities and interventions, FemTech.dk is about extending and embracing the field of computer science, allowing for people with diverse backgrounds and interests to see themselves as successful within the field.

Computer science is the foundation for how new information technologies are designed, developed, and introduced into peoples' lives. Digital technologies shape society, life, and work in important ways globally and locally, influencing how people think and act with technology in all aspects of life. Focusing on Europe, and specifically Denmark, we use digital technologies when we work, when we interact with governments and other institutions, when we engage with friends and family – and when our children engage with other children. We use technology in transportation, in manufacturing, in healthcare, and in unemployment services (Boulus-Rødje 2018; Nielsen and Møller 2020; Boulus-Rødje and Bjørn 2021). We use technology to track illness, energy, or politics (Boulus-Rødje and Bjørn 2015; Møller et al. 2021a, b). Digital technologies are pervasive and ubiquitous. This means that the people who create them influence our lives in important ways. Computer scientists have the power to invent, design, and create the digital technologies that shape our society. "With great power – comes great responsibility" (quoting the popular adage, which is also included in the DIKU student songbook, department song: *Tomorrow the world is ours*).

A large responsibility of computer scientists is thus to ensure that digital technologies that are developed enable the potentials of *all* individuals, communities, and societies; and to notice when important aspects of human interaction are neglected, constrained, or simply missing representation in technology design. To embrace this responsibility, societies would benefit from a situation where computer scientists with diverse backgrounds, perspectives, and ideas are available and can participate in the important task of shaping society though technology.

FemTech as Long-Term Endeavor

Making fundamental long-term change is evidently not a short-term endeavor. Thus, FemTech.dk is more than a project – it is a long-term initiative, and a sociotechnical infrastructure that collects and interlinks several projects and activities supporting the long-term change agenda for gender equity in computer science. FemTech.dk reaches beyond the individual projects, and new projects exist beyond this book. At the end of the book, we briefly touch on these other activities and initiatives, but it is important to state that meaningful and authentic change happens slowly and can only truly manifest itself as stable mainstream approaches shaping overall practices if we think 10–30 years into the future.

However, the importance of focusing on the long term does not mean that we simply act blind-folded and cannot determine short-term changes. Throughout the years of FemTech.dk, we reflectively chose to take certain actions and leave other actions behind. Over the years we have developed a set of principles and guidelines which help us make decisions about where to continue and where to step aside. In this book we give insights into these principles and guidelines and hope that others can be inspired in their endeavors for long-term change.

We hope to inspire other researchers, institutions, computer science teachers, university management, and so forth in designing their own interventionist design artefacts and taking actions to unpack and represent different agendas in computer science and digital technology design. The concrete manifestation of artefacts and interventions we have done, and which we describe in this book, are fundamentally based on the Internet-of-Things, micro-controller programming, and makerspace methodologies. However, future artefacts and interventions can take many different forms, since FemTech.dk interventions are highly interlinked with the new digital technologies and opportunities – and these change rapidly and continuously (Schaller 1997). While the digital opportunities will change, we hope the FemTech. dk design principles will be applicable over the long term.

Chapter 3
Interventionist Research

FemTech.dk is fundamentally about combining research and interventions with a focus on making long-term change. Inspired by sociotechnical design (Mumford 2006) and action research (Bjørn and Boulus 2011; Bjørn and Boulus-Rødje 2015), FemTech.dk follows two main interlinked paths: (1) unpacking and understanding the challenges related to unbalanced gender representation in computer science, and (2) intervening and extending the field of computer science to allow for multiple, diverse agendas. In this way, the overall methodological approach is characterized as action research.

Scandinavian Participatory Design & Action Research

Action research was developed as a research method to account for the lack of research methods and insights into a social phenomenon which made it impossible for practitioners to take appropriate action and to consider the results of that action (Lewin 1946). Action research is thus characterized by an immediate problem situation, which requires attention but lacks methods and descriptive insights to solve. The urgency of the problem required immediate action – despite missing methods and theory. Thus, an important part of the research is to plan and conduct interventions – *while* collecting data about the interventions to develop theoretical insights (Rapoport 1970). Moving from social sciences and into computer science, action research has been used as a method for reflective system development (Mathiassen 1998, 2002) or as an approach to information system research (Avison et al. 1999). Action research in computer science in particular shaped the Scandinavian approach to system development (also referred to as participatory design) in the '70s and '80s – where unions and computer science researchers collaborated closely to ensure that new digital technologies entering the workplace would empower employees and not just support management (Kensing and Blomberg 1998; Bødker et al. 2000). In these research endeavors, there was awareness of the politics that

P. Bjørn et al., *Diversity in Computer Science*,
https://doi.org/10.1007/978-3-031-13314-5_3

arrive with digital systems (Markus 1983; Suchman 1994; Bjørn and Balka 2007), and thus a clear political agenda for taking the perspective of workers (Bødker et al. 2004; Bødker 2015) – blue-collar workers (Kristiansen et al. 2018), workers in traditional women's professions (Wagner 1993; Møller and Vikkelsø 2012) – or in general taking seriously work and workers, which are often neglected when new technology is introduced (Bishop 1999; Star and Strauss 1999; Oudshoorn 2008).

The methodological approach in FemTech.dk takes from the traditions of action research and participatory design in the way that we join the interests and perspectives of the gender-minority in computer science with a clear interest in making a change. The emphasis on gender is a methodological decision to be able to operationalize our interventions within the university context; and we consider intersectional aspects as part of our analysis and activities. Thus, we *do* have a political agenda for change, and we are taking a side in working towards an inclusive computer science field and profession. Simultaneously, we are studying the phenomenon of 'gender in computer science' as an entity – as a black box – and that we want to unpack as many facets as possible of this complexity to discover the core foundations that have made computer science gendered as male in Denmark.

Computer Science Is Not Male – It Was Made Male

Historical research has documented how computer science was made male and White in the USA (Ensmenger 2010) and in the United Kingdom (Hicks 2017) – despite the fact that computer programming and software development were done by women and people of color in the early days of computing, and that historically computer science was a women's occupation (Menendez-Blanco et al. 2018; Rosner et al. 2018a, b; Shorey and Rosner 2019). Interestingly, computing began during WWII, while Denmark was occupied – and thus computing as a profession was introduced later in Denmark (in Regnecentralen (Thorhauge 2006)) than in the USA and the UK. As mentioned earlier, the first department of computer science was not established until 1970. These historic accounts are important to understanding the current situations where Denmark, like the USA and the UK, has produced unbalanced gender representation in computing.

Developing initiatives to improve gender diversity in computing has been a continual topic of interest internationally since the '80s (Albusays et al. 2021). Surprisingly, the gender-minority in computer science detected in the USA, UK, and Denmark is not mirrored in countries such as Malaysia (Mellström 2009) or Israel (Frieze and Quesenberry 2015). Clearly, the gendered characterization of computing is culturally determined; thus, a change must include considerations of societies' assumptions and prejudgments of the field and profession. Several initiatives have been taken to transform gender representation in computer science departments; among the most impressive is the transformation of the computer science department at Carnegie Mellon University in Pittsburgh, Pennsylvania, USA. Here, long-term initiatives and efforts transformed the gender representation toward 50/50 men and women in the computer science student population from 1995 to 2020 (Margolis and Fisher 2003). FemTech.dk is inspired by the work at CMU; however, the culturally different structures of university education between the USA and Europe in general and Denmark in particular means that we cannot simply transfer what others have done in the USA to Denmark.

We do not assume to know a priori why computer science in Denmark lacks diversity; instead, part of our research is to inquire into and unpack the sociotechnical structures that form the foundation of computing in Denmark today. We want to both empirically investigate the research inquiry and make interventions that change the field of study while providing additional important insights.

Our Interventionist Agenda

Interventions can be many things and have many different manifestations (Karasti 2001; Vikkelsø 2007; Zuiderent-Jerak and Jensen 2007; Boulus-Rødje 2012). In FemTech.dk our interventionist approach focuses on design artefacts and draws on a long tradition of interaction design research and research through design (Zimmerman et al. 2007, 2010; Goodman et al. 2011; Wakkary et al. 2013; Disalvo et al. 2014, 2016; Blythe et al. 2016; Menendez-Blanco and Angeli 2016; Menéndez et al. 2017; Bjørn and Rosner 2021).

Examples of interventions in FemTech.dk are hands-on workshops and public events. These interventions focus on inviting participants to implement design artefacts that we had carefully designed to engage and produce certain characteristics about computer science. Our intention was that, when used in interventionist activities, the artefacts would manifest the assumptions and narratives that challenge existing pre-determined understandings of computer science. One important feature of the FemTech.dk design artefacts is that interventions are not only manifested in implementing a final 'artefact' – they are being produced *in and through* the design activities that lead to the final artefact. Thus, the *intervention* is about both developing a *product* and engaging in a *process* – and includes considerations for who are included in our design process as well as the participants invited for events and how participants shaped the narrative of the artefacts. Thinking about design artefacts as a process forces us to consider and to not only collect data about our interventions when the final artefacts are displayed but, more importantly, to *collect data about the process* by which an artefact becomes *made and enacted during events* by participants joining in the events.

When we intervene, we use design artefacts not to solve a need or problem; instead, we used them as a contextual feature shaping our interventions by challenging basic assumptions about computer science. For example, the design artefacts challenged the assumptions that digital technology centers around screen or keyboard interaction or that computer science is an individual activity rather than a cooperative one. FemTech.dk for design thus comprises a conceptual framework that manifests our embedded agenda about change in computer science. We do this by depicting and displaying the interventionist agenda when inviting participants to engage with our proposed agenda, which often means challenging their own basic assumptions about computer science. We used the FemTech.dk events and workshops as a vehicle for interventions, as they provided us a way to engage with different audiences. While we attempt to challenge different kinds of assumptions in different types of ways with different audiences, all the design artefacts fundamentally served the same purpose: to challenge basic assumptions about technology design, the design materials, and the people who make technologies.

Our interventionist agenda includes thinking about the issue as an analytical problem to be explored through design activities. By creating design artefacts that question existing narratives and assumptions about computer science, we can create new boundaries for what digital artefacts might entail (Bjørn 2012, 2014). The boundaries for what make the design artefacts are more than 'physical' and 'digital' boundaries and reach into activities and engagements with people (Bjørn and Østerlund 2014). This approach produces new potential for who can execute interventions and learn about a problem through change. We conceptually designed the artefacts as a multiplicity of strings (Haraway 1987, 1994) for the participant to follow, such as exploring gender concepts within the computer science education and industry or following relevant strings leading into and through the empirical field (stats, documents, stories, narratives etc.), which leads participants to join our production of an in-depth analysis of the problem from multiple sociomaterial-design perspectives (Bjørn and Østerlund 2014). Sociomateriality challenges the ontological assumption that technology and humans are different and separate entities, instead arguing for a relational ontology where humans and technology only can be understood as mutually entangled (Haraway 1990; Barad 2003; Suchman 2007; Orlikowski and Scott 2008; Bjørn and Markussen 2013; Law and Singelton 2014). Sociomaterial-design brings this relational ontology into the design of artefacts by explicitly designing digital technologies with open-ended boundaries (Bjørn 2012; Bjørn and Østerlund 2014). In FemTech we embrace our work as sociomaterial-design.

Our Role as Researchers

We are women and computer science researchers studying gender in computer science, and thus we are part of the phenomenon we study. Studying our own organization as insiders raises specific challenges (Blomberg et al. 1993; Kensing and Blomberg 1998; Blomberg and Karasti 2013), increasing the demand for reflexivity by us as researchers. Being situated as insiders risks blinding us to invisible structures and taking for granted assumptions that we as insiders encounter in the organization. To account for these challenges, we have explicitly addressed our own assumptions and tacit knowledge about the field as part of the research process. A crucial part of this reflection has been done when reading about gender, feminism, and equity in computing and challenging our experiences with insights from existing literature. Also, working on the project meant that we were exposed to, and engaged with, discussions, events, and people we would not have engaged with otherwise. Our discussions about designing the activities, writing papers, publishing in news media, and understanding the feedback on our work have also contributed to our reflections on feminism and computing. At the same time, coming from *within* the phenomenon of study also gives us unique access to and engagement with the field, making the long-term effects of our work more sustainable.

In this way, our methodological approach, combining action research and design research into interventions driven by the design process and final design artefacts, is our way of combining activism and research – of learning about gender and equity in computing while creating interventions – of pushing the research forward by reflecting on results and challenging our own assumptions and lived experiences.

Chapter 4
Makerspace Methodologies & Design Principles

The *four FemTech design principles* which underscore all our work are that design artefacts must (1) produce alternative narratives of computer science, which (2) challenge the taken-for-granted assumptions about computer science, by (3) embedding a story into the design while (4) allowing for surprising interactive opportunities. However, before we dive into the details of these principles, we contextualize the principles in the design practices by which they were made.

Makerspace Methodologies

FemTech.dk is fundamentally about unpacking the phenomenon of gender representation in computer science, with the aim of creating interventions through design artefacts. Thus, the process by which the design artefacts are produced is important for understanding our work – a design process guided by the FemTech.dk design principles that form the basis of our artefacts.

In this chapter, we provide more details about the contextual design situations in which we have worked. These design situations were characterized by technological choices, physical spaces, and events. Then, we introduce the design principles that serve as the foundations for our work. We hope that both the contextual situations and the design principles can assist others in creating their own initiatives and interventions, transforming gender representation in computing.

First, it is important to state that when we began our work, we shared an interest in creating design artefacts that combined physical and digital properties – and we were inspired by the amazing work of researchers such as Daniela Rosner, Nadya Peek, Morgan Ames, Silvia Lindtner, Amanda Williams, Leah Buckley, Audrey Desjardin, Shaowen Bardzell, and Verena Fuchsberger, to mention just a few (Buechley et al. 2008; Bardzell et al. 2012; Tanenbaum et al. 2013; Wakkary et al. 2013; Ames et al. 2014; Rosner et al. 2014; Fox et al. 2015; Fuchsberger et al. 2015, 2016; Peek et al. 2017; Rosner et al. 2018a, b). Each of these researchers has their

© The Author(s) 2023
P. Bjørn et al., *Diversity in Computer Science*,
https://doi.org/10.1007/978-3-031-13314-5_4

own individual ways of creating their unique and novel research, yet they share a dedication to understanding design practices in various contexts, places, and communities – and have in important ways influenced how we can think and practice design and development of digital technologies, as well as how to make creative spaces (e.g., makerspaces, and fablabs) and artefacts that demonstrate counter-political concerns and challenging narratives.

Our research interest aligns well with the above agenda, and part of our work has focused on creating a space – a makerspace – at the university. The vision for the makerspace was to have a place both that could drive change for the perception of computing but also where we could work with participants and students, inviting them into the interventionist activities of design.

UPCH Makerspace as a Concept

In 2016 there was no makerspace or anything similar at the University of Copenhagen, so one of the first initiatives was to see whether we could pilot a MakerWeek as part of our teaching in Fall 2016 and use the insights to mobilize diverse researchers across the university in 2017 to see what we could accomplish (Bjørn and Hornbæk 2017). Simultaneously, we identified all the makerspaces, hackerspaces, fablabs, and so forth located in the Copenhagen area at that time to see which connections we could make outside the university as well (Lundberg et al. 2017; Menendez-Blanco and Bjørn 2019). This work allowed us to define a strategy for conceptualizing a makerspace at the university and to begin as a small grassroots community. We used the UCPH makerspace concept early on to create a Facebook page as well as a website about activities and ideas. This digital presence allowed us to engage in activities despite having no physical facilities. The physical manifestation of the makerspace at this time was plastic boxes with electronics in our offices or borrowed 3D printers which we transported to the SCIENCE library (KUBNord) to set up for the MakerWeek (Fig. 4.1).

At this time, the practical circumstances for engaging in activities in the makerspace made our activities cumbersome and required a lot of resources and flexibility to adapt to changing circumstances. Over the years, we were able to secure a physical space, where we also included bachelor's and master's thesis students in our efforts. The space began as a shared space between Computer Science, the Department of Information Science, and the Department of Communication at the Southern campus. We were also able to raise funds to help set up a component library at the makerspace. At this time, part of the Department of Computer Science was also located at the Southern campus; however, the entire department was moved to the Northern campus in 2018. Although we moved our offices, the makerspace stayed at the Southern campus and gained more resources over time. We, however, continue our efforts towards establishing a makerspace at the Northern campus as well.

Fig. 4.1 MakerWeek preparation and execution

While the UCPH Makerspace concept created a physical and digital context for our design practices, what was even more important was that in our work we wanted to challenge the assumptions and characteristics of computer science as a field, profession, and practice that were centered around screens and keyboards. We wanted to find new ways to demonstrate how computer science and the artefacts produced could be interactive by mixing digital and physical materials. We wanted to move the representation of computer science from a practice directed at creating digital applications for use on traditional digital devices such as smartphones, tablets, laptops, or desktops to exposure as a practice that can also engage in creative design practices embedding technology in the physical world. Such representations indeed exist, but they were not visible initially in the computer science narrative at our university. We wanted to change how computer science is perceived at the University of Copenhagen: not solely as a desktop activity but also requiring lab facilities. Thus, a core design decision we made early on was to focus our technology choices on micro-controllers and electronics – since this allowed us to clearly create artefacts combining digital and physical functionalities and thereby challenge the predominant narrative of computer science in our institution.

Micro-controllers are small computers, such as Arduino, that can be embedded in physical materials, such as textiles, and connected with other devices or the Internet. To allow for extended potentials for designing interactions, we decided to work with Internet-enabled micro-controllers; this choice enabled us to center our design artefacts on the technological concept of the Internet-of-Things (IoT). Concretely, we explored the different technical opportunities and ended by choosing the ESP8266 micro-controller (SparkFun Thing Dev Board ESP8266) as our main micro-controller. The ESP8266 was chosen because of its size, price, and robustness – and because programming could be done using the well-documented Arduino IDE (Fig. 4.2).

In designing the interaction of the artefacts, we also wanted to explore and play around with materials and physical interactions that challenged ordinary touch-screen and keyboard interactions. This made us explore and experiment with different materials such e-textiles and origami paper, as well as different kinds of interaction sensors and actuators such as motion sensors, accelerometers, and

Fig. 4.2 Arduino experimentation

gyroscopes. These different electronics became the technological foundation for our activities both for the FemTech.dk design artefacts and for the opportunities we created for students to join the makerspace.

Similar to the FemTech interventions, our purpose when creating design artefacts is not only to develop an artefact but also to reflect the FemTech principles in *the process* by which artefacts are created. Thus, having a makerspace concept allowed us to invite participants to join our design activities and take part in locally producing new perspectives on computer science. Having a makerspace was especially important for the ways we ended up designing the activities. The main activities we developed were the FemTech.dk workshops, the public events, and the conceptual work for the later kick-starter course for new computer science students created by our colleague Martin Dybdal.

Concrete Interventions

We conducted the first FemTech workshop in April 2016, and since then the workshops have been a yearly event. Since 2018 the workshops have been mainstreamed, developed, and organized by other people in the department based on the same principles. Further, participation has expanded, and in 2021, the workshop was held online because of the COVID-19 pandemic and was open to more than 100 participants invited from all high schools in mainland Denmark, Greenland, and the Faroe Islands.

The kick-starter course was introduced in 2018 as a voluntary opportunity for new students who had just been accepted to the bachelor's degree program in computer science. Enrolled students are invited for a two-week intensive kick-starter course where they learn basic programming and get to know other students. One motivation for the course was to address the empirical observation that while Danish 15-year-old school youth have *the same level* of ICT skills and competences based on actual accomplishments, Danish girls still assess their own skills as lower than boys (Bundsgaard et al. 2018). This mean that the difference between young girls' *actual* computing skills and *perceived* computing skills risks impacting youth choice, since they might question whether they can succeed if pursuing an education in computer science. By offering a kick-starter course specifically aimed at new bachelor's students without prior programming experience, we wanted to demonstrate that one can start and be successful in the program without such experience. The course was open to everyone, and its structure was designed to foster collaboration and engagement between students.

The kick-starter course is a returning event and has grown in enrollment; in 2021, 120 students joined of the more than 400 students enrolled in the computer science bachelor's program. The course builds on the same principles as the FemTech workshops. Further, we are currently discussing how to bring the same principles to ordinary teaching in the computer science program, and dedicated, hands-on

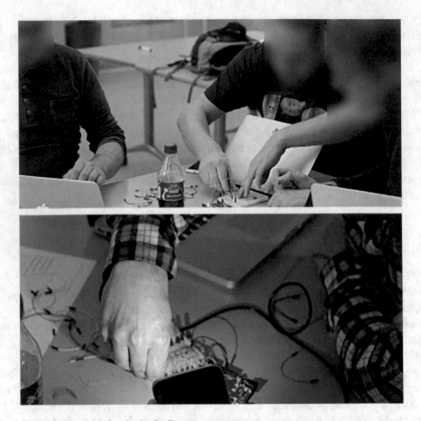

Fig. 4.3 Workshop with faculty in the Department

activities have been held with the members of the department to demonstrate their possibilities (Fig. 4.3).

It is beyond our scope here to explore the details of the kick-starter course or current efforts to be included in ordinary teaching; however, what is important is that ideas and concepts developed as part of FemTech are moving beyond FemTech activities, and efforts are invested in normalizing the principles for ordinary teaching in computer science. In the following chapters, we focus on the details of three FemTech design artefacts: Cyberbear, Cryptosphere, and GRACE; however, before we turn to these, we want to make explicit the design principles.

The Four FemTech Design Principles

The *four FemTech design principles* stipulate that design artefacts must (1) challenge the taken-for-granted assumptions about computer science and (2) produce alternative narratives of computer science, by (3) embedding a story into the design while (4) allowing for interactive opportunities that trigger curiosity. Let's unpack each of these.

Challenging Taken-for-Granted Assumptions

Design artefacts must challenge the taken-for-granted assumptions about computer science in the local context. The first principle guides the design process to explicitly address taken-for-granted assumptions about computer science in the specific context of intervention. Such assumptions about computing can take many different forms, and in our case the focus for our designs has been on *materials* and *interaction*. The materiality of computing artefacts is often viewed as merely digital, as these are structured as 0 s and 1 s. Interestingly, digital online artefacts (such as e-books, gaming worlds, and interactive websites) are not solo digital entities but instead depend on material properties and physical infrastructure such as fiberoptic cables and server farms (Dourish 2017), and we wanted to make these physical properties visible in our digital design. We wanted to emphasize the physical experience of digital interaction through physical manifestation in the artefacts. This meant that when we designed our artefacts, we needed to explicitly and reflectively experiment with and use materials that were often not connected to digital interaction. The material matter that produces the artefacts should through choice of material challenge taken-for-granted assumptions about the material matter of digital devices. Concretely, we experimented with many different materials in our design processes – and in the end each of the three FemTech design artefacts presented in this book are based on a different material experience using different material properties, namely e-textiles, polystyrene foam, and origami paper. By making the material design decision of specific artefacts a dedicated interest in challenging perceptions of computer science, we were able, through the material manifestation, to challenge taken-for-granted assumptions.

Using the same process for choosing the materiality of the artefact, we also considered the artefact's interactive nature. Again, to challenge taken-for-granted assumptions, it was important that the very interaction also challenge existing perspectives of how people interact with computing technologies. We wanted to open the field of interaction by removing interactions from screens and keyboards and introducing interaction as physical movements, soft buttons, or cloud-based representations. We wanted to demonstrate interaction as single user, as collaborative, and as community interaction. Thus, to the design choices of material we added the choice of interaction. Note that we did not select random materials or interactions for the artefacts but instead explored how the choice of different materialities and interactions would be aligned with the second design principle concerning alternative narratives embedded in the design.

Producing Alternative Narratives

Design artefacts must produce alternative narratives of computer science in the local context. The second principle guides the design process by explicitly producing an alternative narrative opposing the taken-for-granted assumptions. Here considerations about representation of residual populations, invisible voices, and intersectional perspectives are important, and choices should reflect such concerns in the design of the artefact, taking into account the specific context where they are to be enacted. This entails that we as designers consider the *activity*, the *technology*, the *functionality*, the *look and feel* together as one. Emphasizing *alternative* narratives means paying attention to *mainstream* narratives in the context where we work, explicitly identifying the *invisible, often overlooked* aspects of computer science, and bringing these to the center of attention. In this work, we are inspired by the research on reflection, inversion, and defamiliarization by design spearheaded by, among others, Senger, Bell, Blythe, Harrison, and Hertz (Bell et al. 2005; Senger et al. 2005; Hertz 2012; Pierce et al. 2015). Mainstream narratives about computer science are many and multiple – and can be related to the practices that computer scientists engage in, how they work, whom they work with, who they are, what kinds of devices they create, what the material of computer science comprises, what kind of interaction is possible, what kind of situations computer science artefacts are deployed in, and why we have computer science devices and products in the first place.

These diverse questions together form narratives about what computer science entails and are locally situated. Therefore, this FemTech principle guides our design towards choosing one or more of these local mainstream narratives and then identifying what has been de-centered or is invisible in them – and then introducing the identified characteristic as the central focus for the design artefact. In our case, a local mainstream narrative about computer science was that technological products are mainly intangible pieces of software (e.g., algorithms and data). To challenge this narrative, we made visible the materiality of computer science through microcontrollers and physical materials. Further, because we applied a do-it-yourself (DIY) aesthetics to the design, our artefact gave participants an opportunity to see 'into-the-black-box' and to touch the wires, the silicon chip, and physical materials allowing for direct visual access to the mechanics of computer science. The second design principle entails that we, both in the process of creating the artefacts and in the final end artefact, must find ways to manifest the alternative narratives of computer science we are trying to promote. Thus, this reflective design process should consider the *activity*, the *technology*, the *functionality*, the *look and feel* as the design strategy to propose alternative narratives on computer science.

Embedding Storytelling

Design artefacts must embed a story within the design. The third principle relates to the sociomaterial idea that the boundaries of artefacts include their contextual nature – and that this contextual nature is part of what makes the sociomateriality of specific artefacts (Bjørn and Østerlund 2014). The contextual nature of our design artefacts depended on the situation in which we imagined them having a function. The situational approach to the context meant that we in the design process wanted to create stories that would make sense in the context given the participants. We had three ways to design the embedded stories. One approach was to identify stories about hidden minorities in the history on computing, but we also wanted to make the stories relevant for participants in the specific situational context. Concretely, one story was about embedding digital technology in mundane objects to enable uncommon interactions; another was based on tracking computer science topics through tangible interactions. The third focused on using interactive technologies to playfully expose an interesting historic event in computing that allowed us to discuss gender in computing. Each of these stories was linked back to the alternative narrative, the material choices, and interaction features.

The embedded story was important in all our activities, since our artefact alone was not solving any problems, did not resemble any ordinary technologies; thus, we needed the context to explain what it was we had created to make it relevant to that context. The idea of making technology that does not solve a problem but instead explores a situation has received increasing attention in the form of design fiction research (Blythe et al. 2016; Nielsen and Møller 2020; Sicart and Shklovski 2020) and different contemporary approaches to critical design (Disalvo 2012; Bardzell et al. 2014; Menéndez et al. 2017; Rosner et al. 2018a, b; Bjørn and Rosner 2021). We are inspired by these approaches in our work to include a story within the design.

Allowing for Interactive Opportunities

Design artefacts should allow for interactive opportunities that trigger curiosity. The fourth and final design principle focuses on the situation in which the artefact is deployed. Throughout our work is the idea that participants engaging with the artefacts should experience interactive opportunities that trigger their curiosity and allow them to gain a memorable experience of computing. The interactive opportunities are related both to the experience of creating and making the artefacts and to their actual enactment. The interactive opportunity can in some situations be about allowing participants to actually make, build, and program the artefacts; in other situations, participants experience an artefact by interacting with it. We have used both approaches – and it is in the enacting of the design artefacts that the alternative narrative and story emerged together with the participants through their interaction with materials challenging taken-for-granted assumptions.

In deciding how to design an interactive opportunity for participants, it is important to consider how the social design of the event becomes part of the design shaping the context. When we want to promote collaboration, we design the event around collaboration; when we want to promote reflection, we design the event around reflection; and so forth. Thus, it is critically important that when we design a FemTech design artefact, it is not the artefact alone that makes the intervention – it is also the complete social engagement design around the artefact as part of the interactive opportunity (Fig. 4.4).

Fig. 4.4 Four femtech design principles

We have now introduced the design principles produced by our work while guiding it, and we next move on to the two chapters in which we introduce the actual design artefacts created and produced as part of the FemTech research initiative. Chapter 5 focuses on Cyberbear and Cryptosphere – both of which were used to create design workshops for young women prior to their choosing to attend university. Chapter 6 focuses on GRACE, an interactive installation produced for Copenhagen Makers in September 2017, to celebrate the 70 years since Grace Hopper found the first bug in a computer program. The GRACE installation, besides being displayed in Copenhagen, was displayed in Florida, USA, in 2018, and Nice, France, in 2019. For the international installations, we re-designed and re-built the GRACE installation at the specific site, while the original GRACE remains in the makerspace at the Southern campus.

Chapter 5
Cyberbear & Cryptosphere: Sociomaterial-Design, Social Belonging, and Gender Representations

As digital technologies are integrated into societies, questions about who partici-pates in technology development become increasingly crucial. When in 2016 we began FemTech, we wanted to redefine the nature of computer science in a way to reach out to people who were not already within the field – and who did not consider or see themselves as potentially successful in technology development. To make such change through interventions, in some of our first initiatives, we sought ways to create design artefacts that manifested alternative narratives of computer science while meaningfully interlinking with people outside computer science. Thus, our interest was to strive for gender equity in computing with an impact not only on educational programs but also on the underlying structures and society, through opening educational programs in alternative ways.

We wanted to enable participants in our interventions to develop critical thinking and practical skills, while allowing us to identify actionable factors to consider when designing interventions aimed at equity in computing with an emphasis on gender. This chapter contributes three analytical and operational factors that are important to consider when developing interventions for gender diversity: sociomaterial-design, social belonging, and gender representations.

In the last 30 years, a myriad of initiatives have tried to promote equal opportuni-ties, diversity, and equity in computing. These initiatives take many different forms: from policies (Mayer and Tikka 2008) to educational programs (Valla and Williams 2012) to after-school activities (Scott et al. 2010; Pinkard et al. 2017). A popular format is short-term workshops (Çakır et al. 2017) and hackathons (Richard et al. 2015; Than et al. 2018). Research provides solid foundations for articulating insights and developing best practices (Duplantis et al. 2002; Frieze and Quesenberry 2015; Tabel et al. 2017); however, we still need more methodological guidance on how to design events in ways that consider the complex matter of gender equity. In this chapter, we report on our experiences and insights in designing and executing such events, and in particular how to develop learning events that consider gender equity, contributing to the research agenda of developing an analytical and operational

© The Author(s) 2023
P. Bjørn et al., *Diversity in Computer Science*,
https://doi.org/10.1007/978-3-031-13314-5_5

corpus of research around learning and education, with an emphasis on diversity and gender in computing (Xie et al. 2019).

Concretely, in this chapter we report on the design and execution of FemTech workshops. We developed and implemented these workshops in 2017 and 2018 – and since then, the concepts have been continued by others in the Department of Computer Science and are now a recurring, yearly event. The FemTech workshop concept is based on the FemTech design principles and has as its centerpiece a design artefact that manifests these principles. The design artefact we developed for the 2017 workshop was Cyberbear and for the 2018 workshop was Cryptosphere. In 2020 the FemTech workshop concept attracted participants for two workshops (24 participants in each); however, the last one was canceled because of COVID-19. In 2021, a virtual FemTech workshop was designed as an online event for more than 100 participants invited from Denmark, the Faroe Islands, and Greenland.

What is important to point out is that the concept behind the FemTech workshop is not simply a workshop to teach young women to code. The challenge of changing gender diversity within computer science *is not* about teaching women programming. It should not be a surprise that gender is not related to ability in learning how to program. Teaching women or other gender minorities to program is not the challenge. The challenge that the FemTech workshop takes on concerns changing participants' perceptions of and narratives about computer science, through practical engagements and skills.

In the last three decades, many initiatives led by industry, organizations, and public institutions have tried to engage more women in computing through different learning activities. A few examples are the Atari Camps for girls in 1984 in the US, diverse sets of IT camps for girls, or Girls Who Code (Kruger 1983; Kelleher and Pausch 2006; Kelleher et al. 2007). These initiatives are instantiated in different formats: from after-school activities to summer camps to hackathons. Most of these initiatives are time-bounded learning activities and, more concretely, activities that seek to foster equity in computing using the short-term workshop format. From a methodological perspective, workshops are an interesting challenge for us in meeting our goal of combining learning activities with an overarching agenda of changing perceptions of computing.

Prior work has demonstrated that when designing workshops that include programming activities, the choice of programming environment is essential. One of the most influential graphical programming languages, Scratch (Resnick et al. 2009; Maloney et al. 2010), has often been used in workshops seeking to increase diversity and inclusion in computing (Richard et al. 2015; Tabel et al. 2017). While Scratch is one of the most popular languages, other graphical programming environments have been used, including Alice (Dann et al. 2006), to teach girls and young women to develop video games in recruiting workshops (Fiebrink and Alcott 2003; Kelleher et al. 2007), and Virtual Family, designed as a "gender-neutral game-based software that introduces Java programming" (Duplantis et al. 2002).

However, in the context of gender and computing, placing too much emphasis on programming environments can lead to an excessive focus on including women in computing as a way to address the symptoms of gender imbalance while disregarding underlying problematic structural issues that caused this imbalance in the first place (Henwood 2000). Therefore, the FemTech approach is based on additional considerations for the design of such workshops trying to make fundamental and long-term changes. Important considerations include identifying ways to minimize problematic situations by, for example, challenging gendered stereotypes (Huffman et al. 2013), preventing essentialist perspectives on gender and technology (Trauth 2002), or considering intersectionality (Armstrong and Jovanovic 2015; Rodriguez and Lehman 2017; Buolamwini and Gebru 2018; Rankin and Thomas 2019, 2020). Indeed, recent research urges researchers to consider that gender cannot be considered in isolation; instead, it should be considered in interaction with other categories such as socioeconomic status or ethnicity (Schlesinger et al. 2017; Albusays et al. 2021).

There are examples where the design of learning activities placed special emphasis on addressing issues of stereotyping, gender, and intersectionality. For example, COMPUGIRLS is a multicourse curriculum that seeks to foster the interest of "girls of color" in computing by reconceptualizing theory of culturally relevant computing in ways that address their identities through connectedness, reflection, and skills development (Scott et al. 2010). Similarly, Digital Youth Divas is an out-of-school program that seeks to create alternatives to dominant representations of computing by creating digital artefacts based on narrative stories (Pinkard et al. 2017). In terms of time-bounded events, StitchFest is a hardware hackathon seeking to broaden participation in computing through collaborative arrangements (Richard et al. 2015). This corpus of research provides insightful outcomes; however, further methodological guidance is needed if we are to increase the number of organizations and institutions that are not experts in gender or educational studies and are willing to organize time-bounded events to foster gender equity in computing.

'Women' is not a singular, mutually exclusive category that can be used to guide design and interventions. Instead, women's experiences are as diverse and fragmented as those of men or non-binary people. Thus, the gender categories cannot sufficiently be used as a guiding principle for design. Instead, we used the FemTech principles. The FemTech principles are not instantiated as recommendations but as guiding questions to aid the design and assessment of concrete activities.

The FemTech Workshops

The FemTech workshops add to the larger FemTech research agenda where we *study* the phenomenon of gender equity in computer science (developing knowledge) while *intervening* in practice (addressing problems) (Mumford 2006). The workshops began as an educational initiative seeking to create opportunities for young women to explore their interests in developing digital technologies and were organized as interventionist activities, meaning that our intention was to intervene through an activity, and then to learn about our phenomenon of interest. Our workshops were carefully crafted to make inquiry into the interests of our participants (Mumford 2001).

We conducted two workshops at the University of Copenhagen, Denmark. The first took place on April 6, 2017, from 9 am to 5 pm. The second took place on March 14 and 15, 2018, from 5 pm to 7 pm and from 9 am to 5 pm. Both workshops invited only young women since we intended to create an environment that avoided replicating gender stereotypes in computer science education as being predominantly male (Cheryan et al. 2009, 2013).

Recruitment for the first workshop was done by approaching 14 high schools' headmasters. Concretely, the first author of this book emailed and telephoned headmasters to explain the project and workshop design. Through the replies of the headmasters, we connected with math teachers at ten schools. We encouraged them to promote students who attended math classes but having no previous programming experience and without showing explicit interest in computer science. This approach was motivated by an interest in fostering curiosity in computer science among people who had not considered computing before. The reason for requesting math skills was that, in case any of the participants decided they would like to study computer science, having passed math classes is a requirement for acceptance into the program. The invitations were sent to different areas of the city having very diverse socioeconomic profiles. We also published an open call on Facebook in a closed group for IT teachers in Denmark and on the university's website. Finally, we reached out in our local professional network. For the second workshop, we relied on these existing contacts with high schools.

In total, 24 participants were invited by their math teachers to the first workshop; only one participant answered the open call. A total of 26 participants were invited to the second workshop. Participants' age ranged from 16 to 22 years (mean: 17). As part of the design of the intervention and the descriptions sent to the high schools and teachers, we deliberatively did not include the terms 'coding' or 'programming'. The reason for this was that the main goal was not to teach participants how to program but to open opportunities for participants to relate computer science to their interests.

Event Design

The workshops took place at the university campus. Participants sat in groups of four and collaborated in groups of two (one group had three participants in the first workshop). Similar to other initiatives (Mayer and Tikka 2008; Frieze and Quesenberry 2015; Sax et al. 2018), we designed the workshops as a collaborative activity to challenge the normative narrative that stereotypes computer scientists as individuals with few social skills, and programming as a solitary activity (Cheryan et al. 2013). We split the groups across the different schools to ensure that no participants had worked together previously (Fig. 5.1).

Fig. 5.1 FemTech workshop events

The workshops began with an icebreaker activity. Afterwards, participants were introduced to electronic circuits and micro-controllers and to the Arduino IDE, which was installed on all individual laptops during the workshop. In both workshops, there were six teachers in the room. In the first workshop there were five women and one man; in the second, four women and two men. In the second workshop we included computer science students as teachers.

To ensure ownership of the code, teachers were instructed not to touch or take control of keyboards, breadboards, and so forth; instead, we made suggestions and answered questions. In this way, all editing of and modifications to the code were made by participants. After a basic introduction, we presented the interactive products. Participants engaged in different activities, which included programming, modeling (e.g., sewing and foam cutting), and connecting the micro-controller to the Internet and pulling information from the server.

After the workshops, some participants proactively organized activities at their high schools. These included a presentation on what they had learned (IoT, e-textiles, micro-controllers) and a video showcasing what can be done using motion sensors and how to encrypt messages on Facebook. In addition, two participants were interviewed by a journalist after the first workshop. The article was featured on the main page of a local newspaper. We joined the presentation and observed the interview (Fig. 5.2).

FemTech Artefacts

The center of our workshops was the FemTech artefacts: Cyberbear (first workshop) and Cryptosphere (second workshop). Both artefacts were inspired by critical design artefacts (Menéndez et al. 2017), as they not only question normative narratives but also propose alternative agendas for the perception of computer science. Let's look more closely at both designs and how they are based on the FemTech design principles.

Fig. 5.2   FemTech in the newspaper

Cyberbear Design

Briefly, Cyberbear is a hacked IKEA bear transformed into an IoT artefact by add-ing a WiFi-enabled micro-controller. Concretely, this IoT artefact allows partici-pants to look up their personal high school schedule online and retrieve information about whether the first module on that day was canceled (Fig. 5.3).

The artefact is actuated by an e-textile bottom (Strohmeier et al. 2017), which participants created and sewed on the bear. The output mechanism is LEDs, which blink according to how the students had programmed the output signal: usually green for canceled, allowing them to sleep longer.

When we created Cyberbear, we wanted to make an artefact that, through its very physical expression, would challenge fundamental stereotypical understandings and narratives of computer science. We discussed the design choices and their rel-evance as part of an interventionist inquiry. The design decision to make Cyberbear in soft materials using e-textiles was meant to shift the idea of computer science as 'something hard' towards computer science as 'something soft'. Thus, by connect-ing digital and analog materials to the Cyberbear artefact, we manifested the socio-material relational connections between what is digital and what is material and produced an alternative narrative depicting computer science as reaching beyond the computer screen – as being more than what occurs in the digital world and including the physical world. The material choice challenged the *taken-for-granted assumptions* about the boundaries of what is relevant for computer science. By bringing in IoT technology through a Wi-Fi-enabled micro-controller design, we demonstrate how programming and creating technology is not limited to keyboard

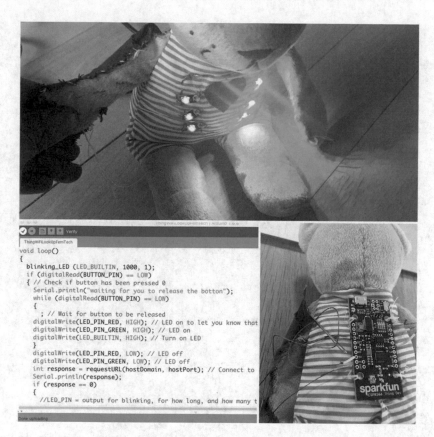

Fig. 5.3 FemTech cyberbear artefact

and touchscreen interaction but includes physical, material interactions. The *interactive opportunities* of Cyberbear also connect the FemTech artefact with participants' everyday lives by linking the artefact to a technology they use every day – their high school online schedule.

Cyberbear was presented to participants as a relevant narrative (waking up in the morning) that has a direct impact on their lives. The purpose of contextualizing Cyberbear within a larger context of critical thinking was to trigger participants' interest in culturally relevant technologies (Scott et al. 2010). The artefact was framed as "Hacking an IKEA bear", since hacking a teddy bear with microcontrollers and electronic components would connote a different activity than one would normally expect to take place within computer science. Finally, we wanted to challenge basic assumptions about skills and expertise relevant for computer science (e.g., as only including programing) and instead show how alternative skills such as sewing to combine digital materials are also relevant. Thus, the choice of *materials* (e-textile, digital, and analog materials) related to the *activity* (to create and design Cyberbear and potentially changing the design expression) was embedded in the artefact and the story about the artefact (Fig. 5.4).

Fig. 5.4 First workshop (artefact and event)

Cryptosphere Design

Cryptosphere manifests encryption as part embodied interaction through movement. Concretely, Cryptosphere is a hollow polystyrene foam sphere, digitalized by a Wi-Fi-enabled micro-controller connected to a gyrometer and accelerometer, which allows the artefact to be connected online while sensing movements as input. As output signals, Cryptospheres have an attached LED strip that reacts based on user input from movements (Fig. 5.5).

Unlike Cyberbear, Cryptosphere is a collaborative technology. Cyberbear is a single-user artefact, where the person using the artefact is interacting with their own profile on a high school scheduling system, Lectio. Cryptosphere is a personal artefact that links to the user's Facebook profile and can be used to communicate with others who have a Cryptosphere using color-coded encrypted messages. The

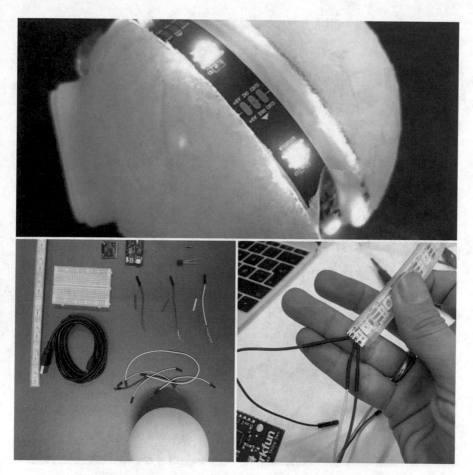

Fig. 5.5 FemTech cryptosphere artefact

interaction flow between two spheres is that a message is written on a specialized message board and uploaded to the sender's Cryptosphere. The sender then creates an encryption code using movement and gestures to set the color-coding of the message: for example, choosing light blue, red, and orange. Next, the now encrypted message is uploaded to the shared Facebook group, for everyone to see. However, to read the message, the receiver must know the color-coding and can then download the message to their own Cryptosphere and decrypt it using the color code. The encryption mechanism is created as a mixture of movements with the sphere, which results in a set of colors (each LED on the LED strip supports 250 combinations, and with up to 12 LEDs you can create multiple encoding combinations). For others, reading and decrypting the messages requires them to know the exact color combinations and how to move the Cryptosphere in creating these, which allows other participants to "read" these movements through motion sensors (Fig. 5.6).

Fig. 5.6 Illustration of cryptosphere use

In designing Cryptosphere, we wanted to link some of the important computer science areas and technologies so that participants could gain insight into the history of the field. Among the important historical events in computer science is the story of breaking the Germans' Enigma encryption and the role of Alan Turing and Joan Clarke in breaking the code. Turing is famous from his historic role in developing the field of computer science, illustrated by the naming of the equivalent of the Nobel Prize in computer science – the Turing Award – in recognition of his contributions. However, less known is Turing's close colleague Joan Clarke, an extraordinary mathematician working at Bletchley Park to break the Germans Enigma code during WW2. In designing Cryptosphere, we wanted to frame the artefact within the history of encryption and link to the history of women in computing by manifesting the practice of encryption through the artefact. In this way, we wanted to give *visibility to hidden minorities* as part of the design. Zooming in on the interaction features (input/output) – the sensors and actuators of Cryptosphere – our interest was in taking the e-textile button from Cyberbear to the next level. Cyberbear had one only interactive possibility – pressing down on the e-textile button – and then all the interaction was driven by the code, producing only the output in the form of LED blinking patterns being red or green. The *interaction opportunities* of Cryptosphere are a complex coordination of sensor input (gyro and accelerometer) and how these are connected and displayed within encrypted LEDs of multiple colors. In this way Cryptosphere manifests how designing digital technology interaction is about far more than touch screens and keyboard input, and thus challenges the *taken-for-granted assumptions* about what kinds of devices and artefacts can be created through digital interaction. Further, the combination of polystyrene foam as the physical material and the digital programmable micro-controllers produces *alternative narratives* about the potentials of computer science. Thus, we combined the story about encryption with an artefact facilitating a cooperative activity using digital and analog materials, thus creating a FemTech artefact to serve as the centerpiece for the second FemTech workshop. Computer Science student Christoffer Belange took part in designing and implementing Cryptosphere and wrote his thesis on the project (Fig. 5.7).

FemTech.dk Online

To facilitate the FemTech workshops, and to support the workshop participants, we decided to use the Arduino IDE and teach participants to program their artefacts using the standardized micro-controller programming – similar to C-programming. Further, we, as part of the workshops, installed all necessary programs, drivers, and so forth on participants' own laptops, and after the workshop all equipment was given to the participants to take home.

In introducing micro-controllers, including installing the Arduino IDE on participants' own laptops and providing them electronic components (wires, resistors, etc.) to take home, we wanted to enable them to leverage their new skills and continue to use these at home. Thus, the design structure of the artefacts allowed participants to continue to design at home – also after the workshop.

We wanted to create a space for participants to continue the dialogue after the workshop. Here the purpose was for participants to share pictures of their accomplishments after the workshop – and potentially to make contact again at a later point. Therefore, we created a closed Facebook group (Fig. 5.8).

We also created the FemTech.dk website, which included a detailed, step-by-step description of how to create the FemTech artefacts, using open-source materials, inviting others to join and use the same concept elsewhere (Fig. 5.9).

Moreover, the website was continuously updated with activities from the research project, including summaries and photos of past events and announcements of future events. The website continues to exist (Femtech.dk).

We followed up with workshop participants though a Facebook page for them only. We asked them to share pictures of their artefacts there (Fig. 5.10).

Fig. 5.7 Second workshop (artefact and event)

In 2017, we also visited two of the high schools after the workshop: Ørestad Gymnasium and Albertslund Gymnasium. At Ørestad, one of our participants presented Cyberbear, how she hacked her own Lectio profile, and created the e-textile button. At Albertslund, two students were interviewed for a local newspaper and presented what they had created. Two Ørestad students also created a video presenting Cryptosphere (Fig. 5.11).

However, other than these immediate interactions, we did not have the resources to follow up on the long-term impact on specific workshop participants. We can, however, see that as the FemTech workshop has developed into a yearly event, the number of participants has increased, and when we asked new students entering the bachelor's program in computer science, several had joined the FemTech workshop earlier.

Fig. 5.8 FemTech Facebook pages setup

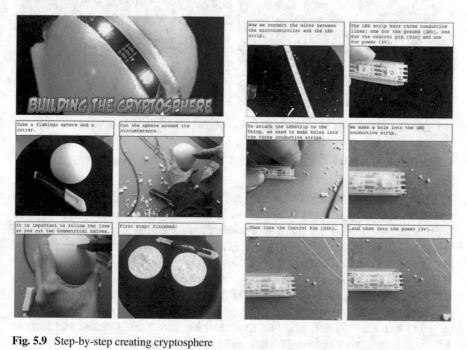

Fig. 5.9 Step-by-step creating cryptosphere

Fig. 5.10 Facebook setup: sharing pictures of cyberbear and cryptosphere online

Documenting and Learning from the FemTech Workshops

The FemTech workshops were documented through detailed, rich observation notes and audio files of participants' interviews. In addition, parts of the workshops were video recorded. Following the first workshop, we emailed a questionnaire to all participants. We received 19 responses. For the second workshop, we email a pre- and post-questionnaire, for which we received 23 and 21 responses, respectively.

Most of the responses were in English, and we translated all material into English and then imported everything into ATLAS.ti. We then analyzed the complete material using inductive thematic analysis. This bottom-up approach 'allowed the data' to guide our analysis and point us to interesting directions (Glaser and Strauss 1967). This analysis yielded 373 empirically driven categories (codes), clustered in

Fig. 5.11 Student presentation at Ørestaden

28 groups such as "assumptions regarding IT", "sewing as stereotypical activity", and "positive opinions towards social aspects of the workshop".

In analyzing the data, we became intrigued by the impact of the design of the FemTech artefacts and activities on students' experience of the workshop. Following this insight, we began to detect patterns in the responses across participants. More precisely, through our analysis, it became evident that there were distinct differences in the way the participants experienced the activities, and that many of these differences were related to the methodological choices we took to make the event inclusive. In addition, the distinct differences were often based on their understanding of computer science and prior knowledge. We found that the responses could be categorized into three main classifications of perceptions and reactions to the FemTech workshops and FemTech artefacts: 'Computer Science is not for me', 'Computer Science is maybe for me', 'I am a Computer Scientist'.

Computer Science Was Not for Me

Although we intended to include only participants with no prior expertise in programming, it turned out that both workshops attracted a variety of participants ranging from no expertise to relatively high expertise. This variety, while not originally intended, gave us the opportunity to explore differences among participants. These results show that the workshop challenged the normative narrative on computer science and that most participants embraced our alternative narrative – but not all of them did.

The fact that the participants joined the workshop through personal invitations by their teachers influenced the group's composition. Some participants claimed that even though they had opportunities to engage with technology in other situations, technology did not appeal to them. Others expressed that their lack of engagement with technology and programming was influenced by their lack of interest in what can be considered the "stereotypical aspects of technology", such as gaming and robots:

> When PS, Xbox, and Wii emerged, my brother was one of the first buyers, as he was a gamer, unlike me. I was not that much interested in video gaming, it did not really appeal me as colours and white canvas did. So, I did not really try anything with technology or programming other than playing some video games. However, I always had ideas of inventing a machine, such as inventing a running machine that convert the output into electricity. [P9, 2017]

What is interesting with the above quote is that after the workshop, the participant expressed a broader idea of the nature of computer science, and of how inventing technology to collect and track running activities could be included in the definition of computer science in a way that was appealing to her. Indeed, many participants expressed being positively surprised about encountering a context different from the stereotypical representations of computer science:

> I never really noticed the computer science education because I believe it is an all boys/ gamers place. Or my prejudice was that only gamers study computer science there to become game developers. But now I have found out that women study there too and people study at [department's name] for many different reasons and not only because of a gaming past. [P3, 2018]

This quote suggests that prior to the workshop, the participant assumed that technology development and programming were not for her. However, the workshop changed that view and, as she also explained in the questionnaire, made her think that it would indeed be possible for her to learn how to develop technologies. The important point for her was that she experienced being able to engage with the topic and be successful.

Working with everyday prototyping materials (textiles, foam) challenged several of the participants' assumptions about computing. More concretely, the choice of materials helped move away from a representation of computing as a complex and tedious activity; instead, the workshops exemplified that it is possible to develop technologies through low-cost and hands-on activities:

> I learned that creative ideas can create new technologies with fairly simple equipment. There are countless ways to use, for example, one LED strip, micro controller and motion sensor to create something. [P4, 2018]

In addition, the choice of using physical prototyping materials (micro-controllers, sensors, actuators) and collaborative activities also seemed to influence the experience of learning digital technologies as more attractive. Working with physical interactive devices challenged several of the participants' perspectives on programming from an uninteresting activity to a creative activity, as illustrated by the following quote:

> Most importantly is that I have changed the way I used to see technology. I learned that technology is not really sitting on a chair and programming for the whole day, but it really is not boring at all! and that one can invent anything and make it come true as long as one learns the basis and have patience. [P9, 2017]

Analyzing the responses from the participants with no prior experience in computer science, it is clear that the workshop design succeeded in drawing interest and providing participants an experience of agency and ability in working with technology, which they did not have prior to the event. The fact that the interactive product was deliberatively designed to bring success after 1 day allowed those who had never worked with technology before to try and not be afraid of engaging with programming or developing digital technologies.

Another grouping of participants had previously tried to engage with computer science but found those experiences frustrating and excluding, leading them to conclude that computing was not for them. Prior experiences with programming classes or events seemed to have influenced their expectations for the workshop. For example, one participant, who had tried some basic programming at school, explained:

> I thought that we would be doing a lot of coding or doing something with computer hardware. I was nervous because I do not have any experience. [P17, 2017]

Indeed, the data suggested that emotional distress prior to the workshop was related not only to the risk of lacking the right technical capabilities but also to the social experiences of participation, as exemplified in the following quote:

> I have really liked this workshop. Usually I am quite shy and do not feel good about meeting new people, but I was surprised about how easy it was for me this time. [P6, 2017]

The workshop was designed to make everybody feel welcome. Participants not only learned new things but also developed a network of contacts across the participating schools. The effort involved in the design of the social structure turned out to be crucial. Many participants highlighted that they really enjoyed the format of the workshop and how it facilitated meeting new people while creating a convivial atmosphere.

The data also suggest that those who had previously tried to get engaged with programming but had dropped out – or did not find it interesting – found especially important that the workshop combined many different materials and activities. For example, one found that the proposed activities tackled many different interests:

The workshop had both: theoretical work and some practical as well, there was something for everyone; sewing, programming, breadboards. Everyone seemed happy and satisfied. [P3, 2017]

The above participant stayed after the workshop had ended to finish the e-textile button. In the evening on the day of the workshop, she also posted a picture of her finished Cyberbear to the Facebook group (Fig. 5.12).

Similarly, another participant, who had reported previous experiences with trying to learn programming without success, appreciated the combination of different materials and highlighted it as one of the strengths of the workshop and a reason for suggesting that others participate in future events:

I would tell them [to her classmates/friends] about the fascinating way one combines soft technology and hard technology and stitching. [P18, 2017]

Clearly, the combination of materials and micro-controller programming was deemed exciting by participants who had not previously experienced computer science as relevant to them.

Fig. 5.12 Facebook cyberbear picture

Computer Science Might Be for Me?

There were also participants who had prior experience at the intersection between design and technology, such as web and product design; however, they did not consider themselves as having expertise in developing digital technologies. Several of these participants reported having only limited technological skills prior to the workshop, even if they also reported extensive experience with HTML and CSS. In general, participants often did not mention skills such as experience with conductive materials, breadboards, and wiring as relevant to developing digital technologies.

The data show that participants with prior and unacknowledged technical skills found it particularly important that developing technology entailed creating something meaningful in a concrete context, where it could serve a purpose. This was exemplified by one participant who had quite extensive experience in web design and found that it was *"cool to see how to incorporate computer science in everyday life"* [P1, 2017], or by another participant, who had studied design of interactive products at school, and thought that it was *"fascinating to create technology and see it 'come to life'"* [P11, 2017]. Similarly, for other participants, programming was not relevant as a goal in itself but only acquired meaning when it could be used as a means to act in the world:

> I have attended a programming camp, 2 workshops and I have tried to study it at my Efterskole, however, all I can do at this point is Lua and basic Arduino. I understand basic java, but I am unable to write it. I want to be able to write code that actually does something, and I hope to understand how codes can interact with machinery to get a job done. [P1, 2018]

For these participants, developing an interactive product contextualized in their daily lives – by checking their class schedule or sending encrypted messages through social media – influenced their engagement in the workshops and their interest in computing. This group of students expressed how it was important to be introduced to theoretical concepts in programming and subsequently be able to instantiate them in a concrete, meaningful product:

> I thought [...] that it was a smooth transition and was pleased to experience that the abstract programming functioned in real life and that we were able to create an interactive product (the cyberbear) with it. [P10, 2017]

These results support not only the importance of learning through practice but also how legitimating skills beyond programming as part of computing is important to making computing inclusive. Shaping the workshop around an interactive product not only supported learning by doing but also prompted participants to think about the use of the product and reflect on it in terms of design and innovation. For example, participants emphasized the importance of considering the product's aesthetic aspects. Concretely, some participants commented on the appearance of the e-textile button, and one suggested that it should be improved so it did not look like "a broken arm". Another student described that she would have liked to work on the Cryptosphere so that it looked like a finished product and not a prototype. Another participant stressed that creating the interactive product also entailed reflecting on design constraints:

> It was exciting to work with the production of the teddy bear, when you still have to think a part of that power conducting wires not to touch each other and so on. [P1, 2017]

Some participants had relatively extensive experience in programming prior to the workshop. Their skills ranged from scripting languages to object-oriented programming. These participants had learned programming at school, had proactively engaged in coding activities with friends, or had used online educational resources (Code academy or Khan academy). Some embraced the workshop activities and the interactive product – especially the collaborative engagement. The challenge for them was that when they engaged in programming activities, they usually experienced the activities as working alone, which often negatively influenced their engagement:

> Currently, I don't do any programming, since I could not find a community or opportunity though I definitely enjoyed it while taking it at school. Over the summer, I briefly tried to get back into programming via 'Hackthissite.org' but it required self-learning a lot of new scripts so after learning HTML and Java I dropped it. As a solitary activity, it wasn't extremely enjoyable. [P5, 2017]

Even these experienced participants explained that the workshops helped them feel more confident about their knowledge and skills. In addition, the workshops seemed to open up possibilities for combining technology with other, varied, interests. For example, some explained that after the workshops, they had become interested in exploring technology with respect to other topics, such as medicine and engineering. One student explained that prior to the workshop, she had wanted to become a medical doctor but that now, after the workshop, she was considering education in technology innovation for healthcare. Similarly, another student described that the workshop made her want to explore the potential of technology with respect to art. Another participant expressed her perspective on computer science after the workshop thus:

> I don't think I would take an education in Computer Science since I'm about 99% sure I want to do mechanical engineering. However, I'm more interested in Robotics as a subsection of mechanical engineering now, so I will definitely look more into that topic. [P5, 2017]

The workshops thus helped reveal capabilities of technology development that participants had not previously considered despite their prior interest and expertise in programming. In this way, the workshops incited participants to think about combining their programming expertise with other academic interests in the future.

I Am a Computer Scientist

The final grouping of students had previous experience in and knowledge of programming and were quite critical of the workshops. Interestingly, their critiques were mostly based on the misalignment between their expectations and their experiences of the workshop. While they found working with e-textiles, foam, microcontrollers, sensors, and actuators interesting and novel, they also expressed that the workshop activities did not match their expectations of what a computer science workshop should be. One such participant expressed how the interactive product of the first workshop was not related to computer science in any way:

> Cyberbear was strangely irrelevant and bored me. It had nothing to do with technology.
> [P16, 2017]

Many of the critical comments referred to the activity of connecting e-textiles together through sewing. The fact that the first workshop required sewing was largely discussed during the activities and in the questionnaires. Few participants thought of sewing as enjoyable. For some, it was a tedious and unfamiliar activity, requiring a lot of time. However, for those who knew how to program and were critical of the workshop, sewing was not only tedious but also problematic because it reinforced stereotypes. In this regard one participant explained:

> I felt a bit forced to be a 'girly' girl when it isn't what it is all about. Maybe a more down to earth programming experience with the hands more into the dirt next time? Try microbit?
> [P7, 2017]

This is somewhat paradoxical if we consider that they liked e-textiles and that sewing is the activity required to combine pieces of e-textiles, in the same way that soldering is the activity required to join metal pieces. If we consider a scenario in which we had used traditional conductive materials, soldering would have been required to connect them. If we assume that soldering can be seen as an activity traditionally performed by men, we might speculate whether participants would have felt forced to be a 'manly' girl? Alternatively, the empirical observations reflect a larger concern, namely that participants wanted to experiment with activities that are "gendered", because they wanted to escape the narrow script of their gender roles and try something either "neutral" or "opposite". In this way, their expectation for the workshop might be that they wanted to be exposed to a narrative opposite of expectations, and then they felt forced into a script they were not interested in.

Moreover, the data revealed different assumptions regarding computer science and what is – and is not – included. It is interesting that the normative narrative about computer science influences the criticisms. Indeed, participants' answers to the questionnaires revealed assumptions regarding their perspectives on computer science, as illustrated in the following quote:

> I was already interested in IT, and was already considering studying IT or something like it at a university. My opinion has not changed since the workshop, but I am pretty certain, that if I had known little about IT before the workshop, my interests wouldn't have changed for the better since the workshop didn't really show a good side of IT. [P13, 2017]

Note that what some participants believed qualified as proper, or improper, is linked to their references to previous skills or assumptions. The data suggest that the stereotypical narrative of computing made them differentiate between what was part of computer science and what was not. For this group, designing situated technologies was considered outside "proper" computer science, as illustrated in the following quote:

> I was already considering it [studying computer science] and I do not feel that this was a proper introduction to computer science itself, more of an introduction to interactive design and how to incorporate technology into everyday situations. [P1, 2018]

It is crucial to note that while the workshops were inclusive in terms of inviting new participants, who had not previously seen themselves as fitting in, the format also challenged the normative narrative on computer science, which risked pushing away participants who already subscribe to the existing narrative. Thus, by pushing for one type of inclusion, we risked excluding others. Indeed, some participants subscribing to the normative narrative had different expectations for what inclusion would look like:

> I think my expectation was more like 'We are going to make some killing- zombies-videogame or something' and kind of get the boy/girl differences and expectation according to IT away. [P2, 2017]

The above perspective clearly reinforces the normative narrative that technology is about 'killing-zombies-videogames'. Interestingly, it also provides us new insights into how some participants had different perspectives on inclusion: namely, that inclusive participation entails supporting minorities to become part of the normative representation – without questioning the fundamental structures. This group of students had already experienced computer science as an attractive domain, and their challenge was related to fitting in to the existing social and cultural structures. These might be examples of the few (the 7–9%) who already choose an education in computer science at the university.

These results suggest that even though this group of young women represent a minority in computer science, it is not an excluded minority in terms of interest. Instead, the exclusion they experience is linked to the gender expectations they meet when trying to fit in. They wanted to develop 'zombie games' and get rid of the 'boy/girl' expectations they had experienced. This insight also highlights that making the field of computer science more inclusive by relying on minorities within the field experiences risks posing limitations. Actually, the results suggest that their efforts in making themselves fit in to the field might place them in a defensive mode, insisting on the normative narrative, and therefore refusing change.

Embracing Alternative Agendas

The FemTech workshops succeed as a scaffold for designing time-limited events that help participants engage with technology design while being challenged on basic assumptions about computer science. In both workshops, all participants managed to create, build, and implement a FemTech artefact – either Cyberbear or Cryptosphere – successfully. Moreover, all participants managed to install all drivers and the Arduino IDE on their personal laptops, which meant that they had the technical resources if they choose to change anything in the code or re-mix it later.

We structured the workshops so that even though each participant made their own FemTech artefact, they worked in groups of two and were introduced to pair programming as a working method. This focus on the social element in technology development was an important feature of the workshop, as part of the purpose was to begin socializing participants into considering that they themselves might be able to achieve and work together on the kinds of agendas they find interesting – and that technology design could be a potential element in this.

Most participants did not know each other prior to the workshop, and we wanted to support all in experiencing a belonging – also in case some participants afterwards might want to continue in any of the computer science degrees around Denmark – knowing others from different high schools who might do the same and that being able to reach out would be supportive.

The first workshop took place on 1 day, and we experienced that the program was long, leaving little time for breaks – and since we wanted to include socializing, we extended the second workshop for one evening, and then 1 day. The evening before the actual workshop took place as a socializing event with food combined with installations of software and drivers. This turned out to be time well spent. It also meant that we could begin directly on the content the next morning.

Introducing the workshop format initially for the participants included introducing them to the FemTech artefact they were to create. This included the story behind the artefact – and here a simple story (like sleeping late) was easier to convey than the history of encryption, since participants were eager to simply begin building and programming. The narratives around the design artefacts are important because this is what makes it engaging and potentially challenging of participants' previous perceptions. However, finding ways to display and manifest the alternative narratives as part of the crafting and making of the artefacts works better. We also found that the DIY aesthetic of the artefacts made participants interested in adding and changing part of the design both digitally and physically – e.g., re-designing the blinking patterns of LEDs on the Cyberbear or decorating the Cryptosphere like the Death Star from Star Wars. These small design changes were part of personalizing the artefacts.

Part of the purpose behind the design of the FemTech workshop was for participants to learn through experimenting and examples – and then to reflect on their experiences as potential future ideas for how technology could be used in novel ways. Since time was short during the first workshop, there was not really time to reflect together – however, we could see in the follow-up questionnaires reflections on the potential use of technology in diverse domains: e.g., one participant explained how health and computer science could be combined. During the second workshop, we spent more time on reflections together, and through drawings it was clear that participants drew potential links between their knowledge of micro-controllers and motion sensors and different domains and usage (Fig. 5.13).

Most participants in both workshops embraced the alternative narrative, which we introduced through the FemTech artefacts. However, we also found that our empirical insights demonstrate the diverse and fragmented nature of women's experiences, where not everyone experiences computer science as an alien culture (Sproull et al. 1984). Women are not a distinct group sharing all the same features, characteristics, and interests. Instead, women – like all other genders – have different interests and concerns. This points to the importance of creating and demonstrating the wide variety of potential narratives that exist in parallel and simultaneously. However, since there are specific gender minorities in computer science, it is important to make extra efforts to actively not exclude minorities and favor the majority. Further, these insights are not narrowly linked to gender but instead apply to all kinds of diversity dimensions. When we facilitate welcoming a minority, we also facilitate people from majority groups but with different interests fitting in. Based on our experiences, we propose three main considerations that can help guide the design of events and activities to foster equity in the very design.

Fig. 5.13 Femtech workshop, second workshop

These are sociomaterial-design, social belonging, and gender representations (see Table 5.1). Let's consider each in turn.

Sociomaterial-design includes considerations of how participants comprehend the boundaries of the domain of computer science and its impact and potential reach in the outside world. Designing activities where you learn about technology for the sake of technology is interesting and engaging for participants who already have an interest in technology; learning about culturally relevant technologies can be engaging for participants without such pre-existing interest. However, previous research has highlighted tensions between culturally relevant approaches and traditional approaches to skills development (Enyedy and Mukhopadhyay 2007; Tissenbaum et al. 2019), such as programming or coding. In our experience, seamlessly creating learning activities that combine reflective activities on the societal impact of technology and low-level programming exercises is difficult. Our workshops show promise for how the digital-analog artefact approach is one way to combine the two. Creating specific artefacts, which include design activities in combination with programming, can extend the definition of computing while allowing for diverse interests. For example, the design of the Cryptosphere (storytelling, materiality) introduced privacy issues of protocols while embedding practical exercises to control sensors and actuators.

Sociomaterial-design also includes considerations of which types of domains are used in concrete examples as well as in a general teaching approach (Scott et al. 2010). These decisions entail considering whether to include domains that can be easily recognized as relevant for computer science (e.g., video games) or other types of examples that are less obvious but equally relevant (e.g., biology, art). If we had made the participants create a zombie-killing game, we would have confirmed the

Table 5.1 Factors and guiding questions that provide methodological guidance when designing workshops to foster gender equity

Sociomaterial-design Participants' definitions of the boundaries of the computer science domain and its impact and potential reach in the outside world.	How are the activities/artefacts presented in the description of the event? To what extent do the activities focus on skill development (e.g., programming)? To what extent do the activities support critical thinking (e.g., design considerations, culturally relevant computing)? What initiatives at the structural and cultural levels can help legitimate the activities in computing?
Social belonging The impact of prior positive or negative social experiences with computer science.	How are participants recruited to the event (personal invitations, teachers' mediation)? How does the design of the event support collaboration (activities design, didactic method)? Which types of domains are used in examples? How does the design of the event help participants connect after the event (social media, follow-up events)?
Gender representations The gendered connotations embedded in the design of the event such as dynamics, artefacts, and materials.	How do the criteria for inviting participants consider gender and intersectionality (women-only event, different socioeconomic backgrounds)? How does the choice of materials relate to gender? Are the functionalities or materiality of the artefacts gender-laden? Does the artefact design allow different gender representations? How is gender considered in the design of the event (selection of teachers, choice of pictures)?

expectations of some of our participants by confirming their bias towards what belongs in computer science. However, challenging the normative narrative, and proposing an alternative, allowed us to open up the domain to be relevant for other participants who are currently excluded from the gaming narrative as a computer science domain.

Interestingly, after the workshop all participants found themselves potentially included in technology development, although in different ways. Most participants embraced the alternative narrative introduced at the workshop. Thus, their technological perspectives extended the definition of computer science to include various parameters, such as different types of use (sleeping longer in the morning, encrypting messages on social media), different kinds of materials (e-textiles, polystyrene foam), and different kinds of activities (design-oriented activities). In addition, they expressed an interest in exploring the potential of using digital technology development to innovate in other domains, e.g., healthcare, art, and engineering.

Some participants refused our alternative narrative and stated that we 'luckily' did not scare them away with our intervention. This was especially true in the first workshop because of the use of e-textiles. Some participants did not enjoy working with e-textiles and described them as too "girly". That some of the participants rejected this material challenges prior work suggesting that working with e-textiles can minimize the sense of 'gender inauthenticity' (Faulkner 2000; Weibert et al. 2014). Our results reveal a complex scenario in which some participants did not want to express themselves through e-textiles, because it was not aligned with what they thought was within the reach of computer science. Therefore, initiatives seeking to open up participation through alternative and critical approaches (Menéndez et al. 2017) need to work to legitimate those activities as part of a broader understanding of computing through structural changes. Otherwise, these initiatives risk designing engaging activities for under-represented minorities that remain disempowered in the broader context (Hicks 2017; Bjørn and Rosner 2021).

Social belonging includes considerations of how prior positive or negative social experiences with computer science matter in shaping future experiences. More concretely, whether participants feel they belong or are alienated (Sproull et al. 1984; Frieze and Quesenberry 2015) depends on the social organization of activities and contexts. All participants offered positive evaluations of the social engagement and of experiencing programming as a social activity. Indeed, the workshop highlighted the importance of collaboration in computing, which can be also considered an alternative to the predominant stereotype of the lonesome computer scientist in the basement.

More concretely, computing is often depicted as an individual activity rather than a collaborative endeavor, and such a depiction shapes the nature of inclusiveness. For example, the extent to which computing is displayed as a collaborative activity displays the value of group activities and discussions and of finding the best solutions together with others. In addition, our collaborative approach challenges predominant representations of success: from individual geniuses to groups of people having complementary skills.

If we want changes in the demographics in computing, it is important to consider the recruitment process for the activities. Concretely, by personally inviting participants, we were able to engage with young women who would not proactively engage with programming and technology development themselves. Thus, we extend existing research focused on self-driven adopters (Buechley and Hill 2010; Tabel et al. 2017) towards not-self-selected participants. Finding ways to engage people who do not self-select is a huge challenge if we want to a have long-term impact. When the math teachers promoted the event as a 'programming activity at the computer science department', the expectations for the activity were not aligned with our workshop design. This could have a positive or a negative impact, depending on participants' pre-existing interests.

Our findings show that experiencing social belonging to an academic field and practice is also shaped by how society embodies certain gender identities in the use of materials (e-textiles, polystyrene foam) and activities (sewing, foam modeling). Our choice to introduce these materials engaged the majority of participants and thus promoted inclusion (Weibert et al. 2014; Richard and Giri 2017). However, the sewing activity was seen as a gender-laden activity; thus, it alienated a minority of our participants, who described feeling forced into a stereotypical gender representation.

Finally, the design of our event as 'women only' was aimed at providing an environment where people felt they could join and be themselves (Fox et al. 2015). This choice was explicitly mentioned and appreciated by many participants, who highlighted the social interaction and structure of the workshop as positive and welcoming. This choice amplifies our interest in change, and it allowed us to explore the diverse nature of the category of women. Still, to be truly open and diverse, future workshops should consider the gender spectrum beyond the binary (Henwood 2000; Vitores and Gil-Juárez 2016). To accommodate this, we in the current call for participation in the FemTech workshops explicitly phrase the audience as open to other genders beyond binary. Concretely, we write: "we use an inclusive definition of women and invite transgender, genderqueer, and non-binary students to join, as well as everybody who identify as women" (DIKU 2022).

Gender representations remind us how choices in the design of the event, dynamics, artefacts, or materials can have gendered connotations. When we designed our activities, we were cautious about whom to include as teachers (Scott et al. 2010) because we did not want to manifest the predominant stereotype that men know about technology (as teachers) and women know less about technology (as students). Thus, when inviting teachers, it was very important to us that most of the teachers were aware of these sensitivities. The leading teacher was a woman full professor demonstrating that women can also be successful computer scientists. It is critical to carefully consider which gender roles and stereotypes are introduced and embedded within the structure and context of the inclusive interventions.

Gender identity played an important role for the participants in our workshop, who also displayed their experiences in their individual descriptions of having a particular gender (girly-girl and boyish-girl). We gained insights into what these gender types entailed for the participants and how they shaped the ways in which participants performed their gender through their appearance and actions (Cheryan et al. 2009, 2013). When participants rejected or embraced the sewing activity, the main issue they expressed was that sewing was a feminine activity, which they refused, rather than seeing sewing as an activity of 'attaching materials.'

Our findings support prior studies of the gender transformation in computer science in higher education, which show that the essentialist approach to gender cannot explain the lack of diversity in computer science (Henwood 2000; Frieze and Quesenberry 2015). Our findings thus confirm that the gender imbalance in computer science education has nothing to do with the biological sex of students, and everything to do with structures and norms of the academic field and education in society.

Moving from gender binaries to gender representation, we need to consider how diverse gender categories extend the ways in which we design and evaluate inclusive and exclusive mechanisms. So, the question is: Did we manage to produce such an inclusive environment at the workshop? We did include participants who had been excluded in prior situations through the ways we organized the workshop topic, activity, social engagement, interactive product, et cetera. However, we did not manage to create a fully inclusive workshop. As a minority of the participants expressed, we were lucky that we did not push them away from pursuing a computer science education.

Essentialist approaches risk reinforcing the gender divide (Henwood 2000; Frieze and Quesenberry 2015; Bjørn and Rosner 2021) by reproducing existing gender stereotypes. Despite good intentions for an agenda of inclusion, essentialist approaches to gender and diversity might have totally opposite effects. When the results of experiments report differences between women and men, we neglect the role of education and society in shaping how we comprehend gender in particular ways. Approaches based on elements of what is stereotypically classified as a behavior performed by men or women in a certain society reinforce the assumption from this society instead of challenging the very existence of such essentialist classifications of gender in the first place.

Chapter 6
GRACE: Designing Sociomaterial Assemblages Unpacking Gender Equity in Computing

This chapter introduces GRACE, a FemTech sociomaterial assemblage that performs concerns related to equity in computing. GRACE is an interactive installation combining IoT, origami paper, and the history of computing performed at three events in Denmark, the USA, and France. Each event was designed to unpack equity in computing through different types of sociomaterial performances, while allowing us to collect data about the lived experiences of equity in computing. GRACE is both reconfigurable and relational. It is reconfigurable because GRACE is malleable and can take different forms (reaching out to people who are committed to the agenda as well as to people who are within the domain but not necessarily committed to the agenda) – even though its core remains the same. GRACE is relational because the nature of the installation emerges in use and thus is shaped by the relational connections created through specific use and people enacting the artefact. Through sociomaterial manifestations, GRACE seamlessly integrates the performance of equity in computing with data collection on equity in computing. We argue that designing GRACE as a sociomaterial assemblage allowed for long-term engagement with a gender-equity agenda across multiple diverse encounters and over several years.

With GRACE we wanted not only to understand gender diversity within a specific institution but also to see how we could create an interactive artefact that would produce both encounters that allowed for reflections and discussions on the issue at hand and new insights and data about the currently lived experiences of equity in computing.

Rosner et al. (2018a, b) demonstrate the strengths of exploring the past as part of understanding the contemporary when they, through the core memory project, made design inquiries into gendered legacies of engineering. In their work, they combine stories of women literally crafting the memory core allowing the Apollo expedition to happen (Rosner et al. 2018a, b). Similarly, we explore that past in computing by building on the story of Grace Hopper finding the first 'computer bug' – a moth – in the vacuum tubes of one of the first mechanical computers and use this as a starting point for the development of GRACE (Menendez-Blanco et al. 2018).

© The Author(s) 2023
P. Bjørn et al., *Diversity in Computer Science*,
https://doi.org/10.1007/978-3-031-13314-5_6

GRACE is designed as a critical design artefact (Menéndez et al. 2017) which both challenges computing as predominantly digital, male, and 'hard' while proposing parallel narratives combining different materials like colorful origami paper in the mixing of the back-end functionality of GRACE with the front-end experience through a DIY design (Tanenbaum et al. 2013), where the functionality is open and visible for scrutiny. Thus, GRACE is designed to trigger reflection and help articulate matters of concern (Disalvo et al. 2014), which in our case is equity in computing.

We performed GRACE at three different events: a tech festival in 2017 in Denmark for approximately 300 people, an ACM SIGCHI conference in 2018 in the USA for approximately 25, and an ACM SIGMM conference in 2019 in France for approximately 400. While the performances took different forms during each event, the core design remained the same. We collected data about each performance in different ways, and over time we were able to identify ways to seamlessly integrate the performance with the data collection about equity in computing.

In this chapter, we introduce the design of GRACE and multiple performances of GRACE over the 3 years. We argue that designing GRACE as a sociomaterial assemblage allowed it to both challenge equity in contemporary computing and act as a data collection vehicle, which ultimately allowed us to unpack the contentious issues (Disalvo et al. 2014; Menendez-Blanco and Angeli 2016) of equity in computing and their consequences for peoples' lived experiences in the field. But first we introduce our sociomaterial-design approach.

Sociomaterial-Design

Researchers generally agree that design objects produce distinctive knowledge (Gaver 2012) that reaches beyond what the designers themselves say about these objects. Yet how to situate, translate, and transform design knowledge gained through design artefacts into broader relevant academic knowledge and insights remains a challenge (Zimmerman et al. 2007; Koskinen et al. 2008; Bardzell et al. 2012, 2016).

Taking seriously the blurred boundaries between design creation and design presentation – between designers' intention and peoples' encounters – we want to develop practical and theoretical ways to think about designs as extending creation, presentations, and knowledge production into multiple intertwined activities. In our work we do not distinguish between design production and design presentation; instead, the two are interlinked in our agenda to impact and intervene in the matter of concern (equity in computing). Thus, we need to pay equal attention to our design intentions and staging (use-before-use) and to how design objects are being produced after the fact (design-after-design) through the encounters people have with our design objects (Bjögvinsson et al. 2012). Our knowledge interest is not limited to our design intention; instead, it must focus on the knowledge produced through these encounters. As phrased by Jeffrey Bardzell, Shaowen Bardzell, and Lone

Koefoed Hansen: "*imagine if our knowledge of modernist painting were limited to what Matisse said about Matisse, what Picasso said about Picasso*" (Bardzell et al. 2015, p. 2096). As in art, knowledge produced through design objects is not limited to the intentions of the designers but reaches beyond those intentions.

Design objects are made and re-made through encounters, and knowledge is produced through these encounters. Design objects do not have pre-determined boundaries but instead are *bounded* in the temporal practices by which artefacts are enacted in practice (Bjørn and Østerlund 2014). The design objects we create are not pre-determined but instead must be understood as emergent phenomena where the boundaries for when an object begins and ends are open-ended (Bjørn 2012). Objects become bounded in practice; the boundaries for what makes the object are created in practice. In this perspective, "*bounded has a double meaning – namely to bind together, as in a hyphenated structure, and to set the boundaries for what makes the entity, as in [bracketing structures]*" (Bjørn and Østerlund 2014, p. 9). It is through the encounters that the nature of the design objects – sociomaterial assemblages – emerges in specific temporal entities. This relational perspective on design objects entails that design objects cannot fully be understood as clear-cut entities with clearly defined boundaries but instead come into existence through encounters of a temporal nature.

Design activities become infrastructural activities by which designers situate design objects as sociomaterial assemblages connecting humans and non-humans – as when Design Things (with capital letters) for social innovation produce infrastructures combining artefacts, people, and experiences (Bjögvinsson et al. 2012). Design objects are both "objectified", as they exist in the world as entities, and simultaneously "experienced", meaning they manifest a matter of concern as part of the sociomaterial assemblages through the lived encounters and experiences of actors (Binder and Redström 2006). In adding agency to design objects, the importance of investigating the agency of humans and non-humans is foregrounded (Bjorgvinsson et al. 2010). Further elaboration of the agencies of design objects and computation points out how objects do not exist in isolation but interconnect people, artefacts, values, and contexts, also referred to as "object ecology", highlighting the role of design as a generative device created through infrastructural activities (Jenkins et al. 2016).

Design inquiry in the sociomaterial perspective entails that knowledge is produced through a dialogue between activities and design materials, a dialogue that continuously challenges the agenda in focus (the matter of concern) through the design activities (Binder and Redström 2006; Löwgren et al. 2013). The design inquiry becomes the inspiration for design interventions (Koskinen et al. 2011; Löwgren et al. 2013), and the artefactual aspects of the design become the objects of inquiry producing knowledge. The design object becomes epistemic, as it "*cannot in advance be fully articulated and demarcated. Rather, researchers shape and develop their understanding of the nature of the questions they examine, as well as potential answers to them, through the process*" (Dalsgaard 2016, p. 4992). Objects of inquiry designed to trigger reflection and imagination can take different forms, for example reflective design (Senger et al. 2005), adversarial design (Disalvo

2012), or critical making (Ratto 2012). Adopting any of these approaches entails a focus on eliciting discussions and debate by provoking, challenging the status quo (Disalvo 2012; Ratto 2012), or proposing alternative narratives through design artefacts (Menéndez et al. 2017). Our interest is in investigating how we, through sociomaterial-design activities, can articulate, engage, and challenge matters of concern through sociomaterial assemblages with open-ended boundaries (Bjørn and Østerlund 2014).

It is not only the design object that produces knowledge. Knowledge is also created through the ways in which the artefacts are staged, allowing for different encounters in different situations such as public events or exhibitions. While we quite literally design through construction – as in building and placing physical and digital materials – an essential part of our work includes considerations of how we produce knowledge through material choices, staging our matter of concern supporting our design research inquiry (Koskinen et al. 2011). When we construct and stage digital and analog materials, we shape the spaces and engagements as key means to construct knowledge (ibid). In our interventions, engagements with objects are usually ephemeral and spontaneous, which poses challenges for knowledge construction (Bardzell et al. 2015) and, in particular, for how we can produce insights from such events. Therefore, challenges are a matter not only of "how" to construct knowledge but also of "what" kind of knowledge we are able to create. Thus, our design inquiry research question with GRACE is: *How can we design an artefact that both performs concerns related to equity in computing across multiple encounters and produces new insights about the concern?*

GRACE Design Process

When we began the design process, we wanted to create a design object that would allow us to perform concerns related to equity in computing while collecting data about those concerns. To that end, we followed traditional methods in design research and interaction design. More concretely, we were inspired by design research projects that focused on designing for debate and on eliciting change through those debates such as the Presence Project (Gaver 2012) and the Slow Technology project at the Interactive Institute (Hallnäs and Redström 2001). In addition, we relied on traditional methods and techniques in interaction design such as conceptual designs, sketches, and lo-fi prototypes (Buxton 2010). The design process did not follow a linear path; instead, we iteratively engaged with processes of ideation, prototyping, and reflection.

Concretely, we outlined a set of variables that we considered important (Sharp 2003). Some of these were related to interaction (e.g., *What are the individual task/s that people can engage with?*), to technical details (e.g., *Which kind of components could be used?*), or to design limitations (e.g., *Design a physical installation that challenges traditional assumptions about computer science dealing with screen-based interactions*). For each concept, we collected a set of inspirational images that illustrated the envisaged aesthetics of the design. In total, we came up with six different conceptual designs, including a digital message board, a digital wall of great inventors, and an interactive origami landscape.

Once we had developed the conceptual designs individually, we got together and extensively discussed each of the concepts, assessing their advantages and limitations. For example, we reflected on the extent to which the concepts could trigger discussions among different audiences about equity in computing (*How could the participants engage in discussion? How could the artefact be described? How could the motivation to design such an artefact be described?*).

Simultaneously, we worked on the general story of the installation. Building on previous work that relies on historical events to unpack and reflect on current issues with digital technologies (Rosner et al. 2018a, b; Bjørn and Rosner 2021), we brainstormed on different historical events that could serve as props. Examples we explored were the inventions made by Hedy Lamarr, which formed the basis for today's WiFi technology, or the discovery of the first computer bug, by Grace M. Hopper.

Exploring each of these stories, we selected Grace Hopper's story. While this story presents many interesting perspectives, one specific reason for this choice was that the 70th anniversary of the discovery of the first computer bug conveniently matched the days we had planned to perform GRACE for the first time – September 9, 2017.

GRACE as an Interactive Installation

GRACE is an interactive installation that celebrates Grace Hopper's finding the first bug in a computer in 1947. The installation uses analog materials (paper, rubber strings, and wood) and combines these with digital materials (micro-controllers, sensors, and actuators) as well as IoT technology (people can interact with the physical installation through a mobile app developed for both iPhone and Android). In addition, the installation is visually designed to create curiosity and prompt passersby to participate in the installation through a combination of colorful materials and interactive technologies.

More concretely, the installation depicts a retro mechanical computer with vacuum tubes, powered by eight ESP8266 WiFi-enabled micro-controllers, which allow the retro computer to connect to the internet. Each micro-controller controls a servo motor attached with conductive wires and rubber strings. Upon the rubber strings, participants can attach paper origami bugs depicting the bugs in the computer. Participants can control the movement and blinking LED lights of the attached origami bugs and thus metaphorically 'debug the machine' by using the accompanying (and publicly available) mobile app. GRACE attempts to push the boundaries of what could be considered computing by combining different materials and technologies in a single installation. Finally, there are four different types of origami bugs shaped by different types of bugs – one being the moth – resembling the actual moth found by Grace Hopper.

When exploring the process of creating origami-paper-based bugs for use in the installation, we found that one of the main drivers in the Danish origami community was a former computer science student, Hans Dybkjær. We reached out and together identified four different types of origami bugs that were appropriate for our use. It was important that they look different and be not too difficult to learn how to fold. We also chose four colors of paper to give the origami bugs distinct expressions: green, yellow, blue, and orange. These paper-based origami bugs were also digitized (scanned), and then used as the main characters in the GRACE app (Fig. 6.1).

The GRACE app was designed as a digital representation of the physical installation, and had as its background the same historic mechanical computer that the digitized origami bugs would fly around. The music for the app was created by Peter Bjørn Rasmussen with Lise Dandanel singing as an ambient background, which could run in continuous loops. The number of origami bugs 'caught in the computer' represented the number of paper origami bugs attached to the physical installation. Participants could, by tapping their fingers on the digital origami bugs, 'debug' the system, and the origami bugs will disappear from the app, while moving or blinking on the physical installation. The GRACE app works for both iPhone and Android and was programmed by Kasper Lorentzen.

Fig. 6.1 GRACE folding origami

GRACE Performance & Intervention, Copenhagen 2017

The City Makers faire was part of a larger tech festival in Copenhagen, where we joined with the GRACE installation in 2017. The event lasted 3 days and drew more than 2000 attendees in total. The audience was very diverse and included families, schools, teachers, researchers, and tech enthusiasts. The physical appearance of GRACE took the form of a large and heavy wooden board (3 × 2 m), which took us approximately a full week to build (cut out and assemble the wooden boards, place the background image, attach the micro-controllers and actuators, etc.). We prepared different promotional materials to be distributed at the maker faire, such as leaflets and laser-cut wooden moths. The leaflets were also intended as a gentle introduction to equity in computing and included the story of how the first computer bug was found by Grace Hopper, a description of GRACE, and information about the research project. Further, we carefully curated the physical staging area we had been allocated in order to create a flow between different activities (welcoming area, origami activities, and discussion area).

The performance placed specific emphasis on challenging stereotypes about computer science (e.g., male-dominated, nerdy field, for video game lovers) and proposing an alternative (e.g., digital-analog installation, public event, craft activities). The performance was meant as a playful yet serious provocation: a large wooden board with colorful origami bugs, portraying a historical event about a woman computer scientist, physically assembled by academic researchers from a computer science department.

Exploring whether and how GRACE triggered reflection on assumptions on computer science, we together with a science education researcher from the university, Jesper Bruun, had brainstormed different possibilities for collecting data about the ways in which the performance had "worked" or not. After three brainstorm sessions, we decided to define the extent to which the performance "worked" as the extent to which it succeeded at challenging individual assumptions about computing.

To that end, we conducted semi-structured interviews that included questions about interviewees' background information (e.g., *Do you have any experience related to computing?*), general knowledge of computer science (e.g., *Do you know what computer science is? What does a computer scientist do?*), and expectations about GRACE (e.g., *Would you expect a computer scientist to build GRACE?*). The interviewees were approached after they had left the area of the performance, to preserve their anonymity. They were informed that their responses could be used for research purposes, and a verbal agreement was recorded. The interviews lasted a maximum of 10 min.

GRACE attracted the attention of people walking by. During the 3 days, more than 300 participants approached us and engaged with GRACE. People explained that the colors, movements, and 'artsy' look of the installation had prompted their curiosity. Thus, GRACE's aesthetic qualities were a crucial mechanism for triggering curiosity and served as a starting point for engagement.

In addition, the staging (installation, welcome booth, table for origami activities, discussion area) guided participants through the different activities and engaged them in different ways. Participants included children, parents, teachers, and researchers. Some created paper origami bugs to attach to GRACE, while others interacted with GRACE using the mobile app to 'debug' the machine. Some preferred to learn about the technical details, and others discussed concerns related to equity in computing. In general, children preferred doing origami and playing with the mobile app; adults engaged in all kind of activities. When talking with participants, the story was instrumental in smoothly guiding discussions towards equity in computing. As researchers, we experienced that the story of Grace Hopper helped us connect the performance with the matter of concern and open up discussions with a heterogenous audience in an informal setting.

In total, 57 micro-interviews were conducted and later transcribed. These interviews transformed the ephemeral encounters with participants into small accounts about perceptions of computer science. GRACE triggered reflection on assumptions about computer science; but, more interestingly, they also showed that despite those assumptions, many people did not really know what being a computer scientist meant. Indeed, when participants were asked whether they knew what working as a 'datalog' (computer scientist in Danish) entailed, hardly anyone knew:

> I have no idea, but my guess is that it would be someone who are sorting data, but I really do not know.(…) they are probably sitting in front of a computer. (Micro-interview, Denmark, September 2017)

Then, when asked whether they were surprised that it was researchers from a 'datalogi' department who had created the installation, only a few were surprised, since only few knew what 'datalogi' was in the first place (Fig. 6.2).

The installation succeeded in performing the matter of concern while gathering data about that concern. When reflecting on what made the installation 'work' (Koskinen et al. 2011), we identified three main aspects. First, it was important that the performance of GRACE prompted people to approach the installation and that the activities shaped by the curated staging engaged diverse audiences. Second, it was important that the story embedded in the design object was designed to open up discussions about equity in computing in an informal setting. Finally, it was important that we were able to transform these ephemeral encounters into returns for the project. However, our reflections also highlighted several weaknesses. For example, a key aspect was the temporal and spatial division between the interviews and the performance. This distinction reduced the richness of and insights about our equity in computing, as the insights turned out to be more about the participants' understandings of computing rather than producing new insights about equity in computing.

Fig. 6.2 GRACE at the Maker Faire

GRACE Performance & Intervention, Florida 2018

In 2018, GRACE was accepted as a demonstration at an international SIGCHI conference with approximately 80 attendees. Since it was impossible to transport GRACE's large wooden scaffold by plane to the conference, we created a different GRACE manifestation specifically adapted to the context. The installation was made of cardboard (with the same image on the old mechanical computer), microcontrollers, and actuators, and origami bugs were attached using paper pins. We also shaped the interactive activities differently than we did at the City Makers faire. We staged the performance to focus on opportunities to reflect, discuss, and share personal experiences related to equity in computing.

To that end, we invited the demo session attendees to reflect on their concerns regarding equity in computing, to think about actions that could help address those concerns based on their personal experiences, and to discuss those concerns and actions with other participants. We did not ask participants to add any personal data (e.g., gender, position, country), since this could influence their engagement, especially given that the group was small and relatively familiar with each other. This decision was based on our experience, which shows that equity in computing is a highly sensitive and often controversial subject, where people might be reluctant to share their thoughts and experiences if there is a chance they might be identified.

After, we invited participants to write those concerns and actions on a piece of origami paper, fold the paper into an origami bug, and attach the bug to the installation. The performance included demo-ing the installation, discussing with participants, and assisting them in folding origami bugs – which could be added to the installation.

In total, 11 people wrote on, folded, and attached their bugs to the installation. Several participants did not create bugs and preferred to engage in discussions with other participants and researchers. After the end of the performance, we collected all the bugs and transcribed these for further analysis. Concerns written on the origami paper included personal experiences and struggles related to, e.g., hiring processes, allocation of research funding, and students' feedback, as illustrated in the following quote collected in a bug:

> Students can sometimes be very negative and abuse my status as a young, female professor. Nasty comments in reviews and evaluations hurts the most. (Note on bug, USA, January 2018)

This quote expresses a concern about equity in computing illustrated by a shared experience. Other bugs and discussion included participants' individual experiences, as in a collective diary of anonymously collected concerns.

In addition, some of these individual concerns expressed in the bugs related to themes discussed during the conversations. For example, when discussing equity in computing with respect to hiring processes, a senior researcher highlighted how it was important to consider gender when hiring computing professionals. Relatedly, one participant described in her bug that even though she considered it important to think about gender during hiring processes, such initiatives should be implemented carefully. Concretely, she explained that she had been encouraged to apply for a position at a *'big fancy software company'* because *'there are no girls in the team'*, which she found *'insulting in some many ways' (Note on bug, USA, January 2018)*. This situation demonstrates that even though everyone agreed that hiring processes are important to creating equity in computing, there are nuances to these concerns. The performance of concerns through different means (discussions, anonymous notes on the origami bugs) including different participants was instrumental in producing these different views (Fig. 6.3).

Not all concerns were illustrated through personal experiences; some were expressed in terms of existing studies, theory, or available data related to equity in computing, as illustrated in the following quote:

> I worry about what Lorraine Code called "discrimination by design" i.e. user experiences that implied that the user was a member of an assumed demographic group. We often use

Fig. 6.3 GRACE at the SIGCHI conference

ourselves as our model of a human being. We white men [need] to think outside of those assumptions, so that we stop discriminating by design (even if that is not our conscious intention). (Note on bug, USA, January 2018)

In this case, the concern was expressed not in terms of lived experiences but as a matter of interest for research purposes, aligned with the topics of the conference. This quote exemplifies a participant who is not dependent on the change but is still committed to it (Fig. 6.4).

The performance of GRACE allowed us to produce insights about equity in computing in a different way from the City Makers faire, since instead of holding interviews after the fact, we were about to produce insights about equity in computing from the diverse perspectives of the participants. The insights gave us interesting snapshots of participants' concrete experiences. Interestingly, GRACE as a performance was adapted in a very concrete way, as in replacing wood with cardboard – and reducing the size by more than one-fourth of its first instantiation – however, the

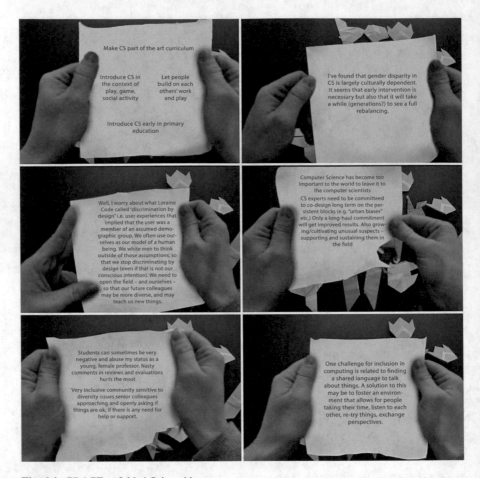

Fig. 6.4 GRACE unfolded Origami bugs

main qualities and story remained the same and shaped interactions and participations in ways similar to the City Makers faire. So, while the physical manifestation looked different, the core story and aesthetic expression remained the same. Moreover, the performance emphasized the importance of sharing opinions and experiences while engaging in discussions by reducing the prominence of the origami activities. Note that while the origami activities were not as prominent as in the Makers faire, they were still relevant because they enabled a playful and convivial setting in which to discuss issues of critical importance.

The GRACE performance at the SIGCHI conference allowed us to collect insights not only as observations but also as actual experiences written on the origami bugs collected. In this way, there was no spatial or temporal division between performance and data collection. However, this activity did not fully match the metaphor of the 'bugs', since the origami bugs contained not only challenges (considered the 'bugs' in the computing field and profession) but also proposals for action.

GRACE Performance & Intervention France 2019

In 2019, we were invited to present GRACE in a keynote at a top international conference in the field of multimedia and computing. The performance was divided into a keynote and an interactive demo session. At the keynote, we introduced FemTech work, discussed the issue of equity in computing, and presented some of the FemTech actions we had done previously. At the end of the keynote, we invited attendees to write on a piece of origami paper the challenges for people to enter, stay, and advance in a career in computer science. Next, we asked them to create one origami bug each (only using the moth origami design linking it back to Grace Hopper's real moth) and to leave these on the table. Instructions for how to fold the bugs were placed on each table, and a total of eight student volunteers aided the task. After all the bugs were collected, we attached these to the GRACE installation, which was made using a pinboard and was much larger (3 × 4 m) than in the two previous events.

Attendees were invited to visit the installation, unfold the bugs made by other anonymous attendees, read the challenges aloud, and discuss the issues written. A voice recorder was placed on the tables to record the conversations. We intentionally did not ask attendees to include any information in the bugs that could identify them in any way. With this strategy, we wanted people to feel free to answer and not feel intimidated to express their opinions openly (Fig. 6.5).

Around 400 people attended the lunch keynote. A total of 154 people folded origami bugs, and 75 wrote down challenges inside them. This performance

Fig. 6.5 FemTech Keynote, 2019

provided a rich corpus of data displaying participants' concerns about equity in computing. As in the previous performance, participants highlighted personal stories and research-related issues. However, this was the first time that participants highlighted issues related to intersectionality, expressed potentially unpopular opinions, or challenged equity being a concern at all.

For example, in the context of discussing the stereotypes and assumptions about gender in computing written in the bugs, a man explained:

> Coming from [country1], the first foreign country was [country2] and I was treated like… "criminals are coming!" But when I said "I'm an engineer" and suddenly, you know, they appreciated me. (discussion, P5, Demo session, France, 2019)

This comment generated an interesting discussion among people who had experienced discrimination in computing because of intersectional aspects (e.g., gender, race, nationality). Interestingly, the discussion triggered by reading aloud the text written in the 'bugs' helped participants adopt the strategy of finding common ground, rather than achieving a unified consensus. In addition, and differently from previous performances, some of the data contained potentially unpopular stereotypes:

> Men are thinking in a rational way while women think more in an emotional way but CS needs people be reasonable… (Note on bug, France, 2019)

Indeed, stereotypes and assumptions occupied much of the discussions during the performance of GRACE, and participants agreed that stereotypes are especially harmful to equity. Interestingly, they talked about not only stereotypes related to a specific gender, and how these might prevent people from choosing a career in computing, but also concerns about stereotypes related to nationalities or assumptions about the skills a computer scientist has, which potentially can prevent people from continuing or advancing in a career in computing. For example, a woman participant expressed that when collaborating in research projects, her colleagues in other disciplines referred to her as "*'the technical people' as if I came with a screwdriver or the soldering station*" (Discussion, P1, Demo session, France, 2019) (Fig. 6.6).

Finally, a few participants reported skepticism about the existence of the concern in the first place in writing on their anonymized origami bugs sentences such as "*I see no problem!!!*" (Note on bug, France, 2019). What we find particularly interesting is that some participants felt entitled to express their opinion, even if it meant challenging the idea of equity as a concern at all, and that our performance managed to engage their views in the discussion, thereby producing opportunities for collective interaction with many different views on a concrete concern.

Fig. 6.6 GRACE at ACMMM

GRACE as Intervention and Performance

Our research interest with GRACE was to perform concerns about equity in computing while producing new insights about those concerns. What made GRACE a conceptual vehicle for different types of engagements and social events were three main relations. These produced the sociomaterial assemblages (Orlikowski 2007; Bjørn and Østerlund 2009, 2014; Østerlund and Bjørn 2011) that made GRACE: (1) a reconfigurable core that was adaptable to concrete situations, (2) diverse ways to engage with both people who are dependent on a change and to mobilize additional people to commit to the change, and (3) seamless integration of the performance of GRACE and the collection of insights about equity in computing.

Reconfigurable Core

While our process was inspired by traditional interaction design methods, our intent was not to create a finished prototype, or a final product (Pierce et al. 2015). Instead, our interest was in expressing the lived experiences, perceived consequences, and desired futures (Disalvo et al. 2014; Nielsen and Møller 2020) pertinent to equity in computing moving towards heterogeneously participation in 'who' can successfully take part in shaping the digital technologies of the future. Concretely, GRACE was flexible enough to be adapted for specific audiences and thus to perform differently during events, while still having a core – an 'installed base' (Bowker and Star 2002) that remained the same. The installed base embedded in the design of GRACE challenges equity in computing through different types of provocations (Raptis et al. 2017). *Aesthetic provocation* concerns the material design, the combination of the digital and analog features, and the use of colors, origami paper, and physical installation. *Functional provocation* challenges computing through the representation of an old mechanical machine with vacuum tubes and how this old computer becomes a novel IoT device that metaphorically allows participants to debug the technical system and the social system of computing. *Conceptual provocation* (Raptis et al. 2017) is related to the story of Grace Hopper and how a woman is behind one of the core concepts in computing *debugging*, even if the field is predominantly male.

While the core remained the same, GRACE was flexible for interpretation across different social groups (Orlikowski 1992; Mark et al. 2007) and in this way resembled a boundary object (Star and Griesemer 1989). However, what allowed GRACE to move across events were the ways in which it was performed as sociomaterial assemblages (Bjørn and Østerlund 2014) – as a relational artefact that shaped the connections between the IoT implementation, the material nature of origami paper, the GRACE app, the specific event, and the engagement with people. GRACE's concrete physical manifestation took different forms in terms of both physical size (from 3 × 2 m in Denmark, A0 size in the USA, and 3 × 4 m in France) and physical material (wood, cardboard, and pinboard). Yet the fundamental aesthetic expression and provocations remained the same.

Thus, GRACE can be perceived as an epistemic artefact (Dalsgaard 2016) due to the open-ended design that allowed it to transform and be shaped through local and situated encounters. Each new manifestation of GRACE became a way for us to enact recursively on the matter of concern – equity in computing – and how this concern was embedded in the core design of the sociomaterial assemblages. Each new iteration included and was defined from the former iterations. So, while future iterations of GRACE might take different forms, past manifestations remain as the reconfigurable core.

By explicitly not engaging in stereotypical norms and cultures around computing, GRACE seeks to produce the field of computing as an alternative narrative combining novel technological components like IoT with digital and analog design. GRACE is a multiplicity demonstrating equity in computing as something that cannot merely be understood as a 'percentage of women' (Bardzell 2010) but instead must be understood from several equally important cultural and social perspectives. These include history, women, technologies, and the lived experiences of people in the field – whether women or transgender experiences of sexism or participants' opinions that there is no problem (as we saw in France).

These insights tell us something about what is visible and what is invisible in the concrete lived experiences of gender norms and stereotypes in computing. In this way, GRACE as a sociomaterial assemblage produces the agenda of equity in computing not as an exclusively women's problem but as rooted in cultural and social phenomena shaping what is seen as prestige in computing in terms of topics and domains (back-end developing system or front-end developing interactions) but also in terms of gender norms and stereotypes. In producing the back end of GRACE as a visible DIY installation with wires, micro-controllers exposed, we produce the front end of GRACE – the human interaction with the GRACE computer as embedded visible part of the back end. Thus, we break down the barriers between what is back end and front end – what is often seen as prestige within computing (back-end development) becomes a 'naturalized' part of the front end and the user experience.

Engaging People Through Encounters

When we engage and produce GRACE through different encounters, we serve two agendas. First, we explore the seamless relations by which GRACE is produced to embody our concern for equity in computing through material objectification of the very issue. Second, we produce engaging encounters situated in specific sociocultural situations. These encounters foster discussions that challenge the status quo by producing opportunities for collective interaction and endeavors. Through these events, GRACE disputes fundamental assumptions about equity in computing through collective engagements (Menendez-Blanco and Angeli 2016) which include different groups of people, some of whom are affected directly by the homogeneity of the computing field and who want to make a change, and others who are part of the producing of homogeneity in the field without such explicit change agendas. In each manifestation of GRACE, we engaged not only those who were alert to the unbalanced gender concerns in computing and dependent on a change but also those who had not considered the problematic issues of homogeneity in computing prior to their experience of GRACE, however prone they were to committing to the cause for change. GRACE as our design artefact seeks not only to engage with people outside computing to get them to join (this would be a project about increasing numbers of women in computing) but also to engage people inside computing to allow them to notice the challenges of equity, thus mobilizing a transformation (Akrich et al. 2002a, b).

By drawing together involved actors, artefacts, resources, and creativity in order not only to manifest concerns about equity in computing but also to involve people who are not currently taking part in the transformation, we extend the group of allies through design (Latour 1987). The artistic expression of GRACE produces meaning as part of the cultural exchange with the participant, which again provides theoretical insights and resources (Bardzell et al. 2015) contributing to insights about the issue. When making real change, it is critical to engage those who depend on a successful change as well as those who do not but are however still committed to that change (Marres 2007; Dantec and DiSalvo 2013). Extending the involved groups allows us to involve people who are important for the change but not affected by the unbalanced gender distribution to engage with and commit to make a change seeking to foster equity in computing.

Seamless Integration of Performance and Collecting Insights

GRACE is about creating change by making artefacts (Menéndez et al. 2017) – since it is through the design we create that contemporary orientations about society are produced (Disalvo et al. 2014). GRACE is about challenging contemporary society to think differently about equity in computing – so that the sociomaterial assemblages we create become carriers of alternative societal thinking. GRACE is not about resolving the issue by design; it is instead about producing a meaningful shift (Rosner et al. 2018a, b) from telling historical facts about Grace Hopper finding moths in vacuum tubes towards a way of collecting and reflecting on lived experiences in contemporary computing. Such reflections are critical to engage in criticism through conversations. A narrow focus on only the historic narrative of Grace Hopper and how well GRACE makes participants aware of the history would be a simply fact-based perspective, solving the problem of people not knowing the history of Hopper. However, this perspective neglects the story by which GRACE challenges the status quo – and produces an alternative narrative (Menendez-Blanco et al. 2018) which is embedded in the sociomaterial assemblages.

Our focus is not whether the situations are resolved through the design (Koskinen et al. 2011) but about creating engaging conversations, increasing the group of committed people required to make a change. GRACE asks questions such as *What does equity in computing mean, and how is it produced in real-life experiences?* GRACE invites people to enter a world where gender homogeneity is pertinent and then to reflect on what *heterogeneously computing* would look like and how it would transform the field and profession.

The sociomaterial assemblages producing GRACE serve as a scaffold and infrastructure for engaging in discussions on equity. The scaffold includes the physical installation (origami, app, etc.) as it is produced through the events' structure and staging, but not only that. GRACE's sociomaterial assemblages function to expose and re-imagine the conversations on gender equity – and thus seek to begin and move the conversation towards transformation. GRACE allows participants to re-imagine through 'prototyping' a new future for computing through their stories on the origami bugs. The GRACE artefact comes into being through participation. The open-endedness is deliberate and critical for the purpose of being not only a performance but also an instrument to provide novel insights into the area of computing.

We engage in the design of GRACE to ask questions while collecting data about the core problems that are pertinent to the matter of concern. We are not trying to solve a problem; we are actively conceptualizing the problem. In this way, we use research through design as a mode of inquiry (Zimmerman et al. 2007). GRACE is about exploring and learning about the lived qualities of the political conditions (Disalvo et al. 2014) that make gender homogeneous in computing. GRACE is a provocation (Raptis et al. 2017) and a method of inquiry – as a way to collect data. Thus, we use it to unpack the 'implicit norms and stereotypes' that challenge gender diversity (Bjørn and Menendez-Blanco 2019). We critically explore what roots have turned the field of computing into a gender-homogeneous field instead of a diverse one.

Methodologically, GRACE is interesting as a knowledge production artefact. Over the years during which we iteratively developed GRACE, its performance became seamlessly integrated with the collection of data about equity in computing. During the first manifestation, the performance and the data collection had weak ties, in that the data were collected through micro-interviews with participants *after the fact*. In this way, the data collection and the performance were two separate activities. During the second and third performances, the data collection was merged into the origami-folding activity when participants wrote down their concerns about equity. The connection between the performance and the data collection became completely seamless in the third manifestation, when conference participants were asked not only to write down their experiences but also to open the anonymous origami bugs and read aloud the text and discuss the issues collectively. GRACE produces knowledge as embodied in the object by combining historic facts about Grace Hopper, through an IoT functionality linked to digital interaction with the lived experiences documented by participants as they write on the origami paper and attach the bugs. When we change the mode from *participation as producing data* (writing on origami bugs) *to reflecting* (reading and discussing what is written on the origami bugs), we also shift from the *subjective experiences to a collective reflection* searching for insights about the issue at hand. We move from knowledge as embodied in design into knowledge as research insights on the area of concern (Bardzell et al. 2016). The knowledge of GRACE is not just about what we, as designers, say (Bardzell et al. 2015) about GRACE but also the manifestation of the sociomaterial assemblage that makes GRACE. The sociomaterial performance of the matter of concern (Bjorgvinsson et al. 2010, 2012) – equity in computing – became completely integrated with the data collection about the concern. In this way, GRACE had a double nature and performed a robustness over time. GRACE was designed through temporal initiations and yet persisted over 3 years. Though the physical manifestation of GRACE might disappear, the GRACE app persisted on participants' mobile devices as reminders of the issues of equity in computing. Fundamental and culture challenges are not simply fixed through one event; thus, designing for long-term engagement is vital however difficult – and future research should continue to explore the temporal and interventionist nature of design artefact.

Who are the champions proposing alternative narratives to homogeneous computing? Who are the advocates for equity in computing? We as designers take on the explicit agenda when we design sociomaterial assemblages such as GRACE. Thus, we are the carriers of alternative narratives (Bardzell et al. 2015). But since GRACE is produced through interactions, participants are invited to become protagonists and thus to shape the future of computing by adding their story and experience to the design artefact. The design artefact is not about answering clearly formulated questions (since if we knew the clear question, the issue of equity in computing would not be a wicked problem (Dalsgaard 2016)) but instead serves as a vehicle for materializing questions and bringing new insights. The design artefact is a way to embody the problem of gender equity and thus to explore the problem as a reflection on concrete realized experiences. In this way, GRACE embodies and examines a wicked problem (Bell et al. 2005) as a way of exploration. The design artefact is a knowledge producer (Bardzell et al. 2015) both for people encountering the artefact and for us as researchers who designed it, since we use it to learn about the lived experiences of equity in computing.

Chapter 7
Equity & Inclusion

When beginning our research on equity, diversity, and inclusion under the umbrella of FemTech.dk research, we engaged with new literature, theory, and analytical approaches from research on equity and inclusion – research we did not know prior to FemTech.dk but which has been fundamental to our activities. In this chapter, we introduce the theoretical vocabulary we have learned as we entered this research space. Our purpose is to provide a short introduction to the most important concepts we found essential and relevant for our purpose of exploring diversity in computer science and to give readers a quick introduction to the most important concepts, which they then can use to initiate equity work in their institutions.

However, we encourage readers who want to expand their knowledge to dive into some of the foundational literature on equity in order to gain much more detailed insights on the complexity of historic structures that challenge equity today (Crenshaw 1988, 1989; Haraway 1990, 1991; Butler 1999; Ensmenger 2010; Ahmed 2012, 2016, Benjamin 2016, 2019a, b; Hicks 2017).

But before we discuss all the important concepts, we begin with a fundamental discussion of technology design which we brought to FemTech.dk initially. Namely, the discussion on politics in technologies – since this argument demonstrates why equity and inclusion in computer science are critically important for democratic societies, and why we urgently need to take action.

Technologies Have Embedded Politics, and It's a Technical Problem

"Artefacts have politics" is a much quoted phrase from Landon Winner's famous paper (Winner 1986) where he uses the height of a bridge to demonstrate how access to a beach can be controlled by preventing public buses (thus, people who do not have their own car) from traveling under it en route to the beach. Bringing the

© The Author(s) 2023
P. Bjørn et al., *Diversity in Computer Science*,
https://doi.org/10.1007/978-3-031-13314-5_7

argument to classification schemes, Lucy Suchman (Suchman 1994) began an important debate about whether such schemes and categories bring in politics when designed into digital systems. Engaging in this debate, Wanda Orlikowski (Orlikowski 1995) demonstrated how classification schemes and categories developed under apartheid in South Africa were very much used to restrict and constrain particular people while enabling other groups in their efforts. Clearly, technologies are not apolitical artefacts; they bring certain values embedded in the kinds of classification schemes that serve as the infrastructure in these systems (Bjørn and Balka 2007). This political nature of technology requires us to pay attention to several questions: Who benefits from the use of technologies, and how? Who are the designers and creators of technology? Where are the designers and creators of technology located in the world, and how do their perspectives, frames of reference, and/or privileges shape the technologies that are built?

So why is this a technical problem? Let's unpack that through the example of designing a dental appointment scheduling IT system for a pediatric dental clinic in Denmark. In Denmark, pediatric dental clinics are part of primary schools, and patients are scheduled for regular visits by the clinic secretary, which includes informing a child's parents of the appointment date and time. So, unlike adult dental systems, appointments are initiated by the clinic – not the patient – and patients and parents are informed of appointments.

Before 2001, all invitation letters from the school dental clinic were send by physical mail to the child's address. However, in 2001 e-Boks (governmental digital mail) was implemented in Denmark, and in 2010 NemID (unique citizen login to all official IT systems such as tax IT-systems, school IT-systems, banking IT-systems, pension IT-systems, healthcare IT-systems etc.) was implemented. These two IT systems together allow all Danish citizens to receive and communicate digitally with public and private entities. While these systems indeed decreased the resources otherwise spent on envelopes and stamps, they also introduced new challenges and considerations about societal classification systems and their impact on the user interface, on the algorithms, and on the database models and tables embedded within such technical systems. Let's dive into the problem.

Prior to the implementation of e-Boks and NemID, all dental invitation letters were sent to the mother of a child in a physical envelope. The letter was easy to share within the household, e.g., by hanging it on the fridge or a shared pinboard – or simply by handing it to household members. However, when the invitations to dental appointments became digitalized using the same classification scheme and 'algorithm' as in the paper-based system, invitations were limited to mothers' e-Boks and were no longer easily shared among household members.

Figure 7.1 presents a simplified database diagram of the pediatric dental appointments IT system, demonstrating how appointments are performed at specific clinics, scheduled by the secretary, and invitations sent to patients. Further, the patient entity includes a number of fields such as mother' name, father's name, and address. The database structure is based on the assumption that patients' households comprise these variables. Now algorithms for sending the invitation use the data in the database but also include assumptions about the household, namely that it is the

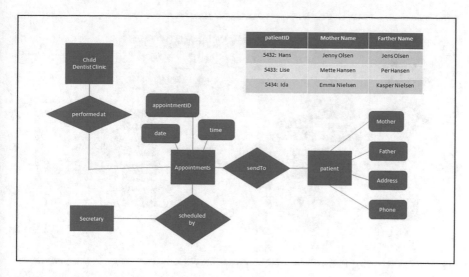

Fig. 7.1 Database model for pediatric dental appointment illustration no. 1 on how the politics of classifications and categories is a technical problem

mother who is responsible for children's dental appointments. This means that the invitation is sent to the mother. However, when the name and address is not just physically printed on paper but is instead used to direct which digital e-Boks the invitation should be addressed to, it limits who has access to the information about dental appointments in the household, which again limits the household's agency in deciding how to organize the tasks.

As concretely experienced by the first author of this book, the change to e-Boks meant that her children missed their dental appointments because in her household she would receive the digital appointments, but in her family, it is her husband who takes on the task of ensuring that their children do not miss dental appointments. For this example, a simple change could be to 're-design' the algorithm for sending notifications of dental appointments to include both mother and father. However, it is not enough to simply change the algorithm since the underlying database continues to create problems.

If we have a case where a mother chooses to raise her child with her own sister, and thus the three are living together and both the child's mother and maternal aunt need to be informed of dental appointments, then the secretary can choose to circumvent the system, using it in a different way than intended by the designers, and simply enter the name of the maternal aunt in the field reserved for the father. The algorithm would remain the same and the secretary would achieve the task of informing both mother and aunt of dental appointments (Fig. 7.2).

However, this would be an incorrect use. Instead, a re-design (see Fig. 7.2) of the underlying database and categories would be more appropriate. Here the issue could be resolved by replacing the categories of 'mother' and 'father' with caregiver1 and

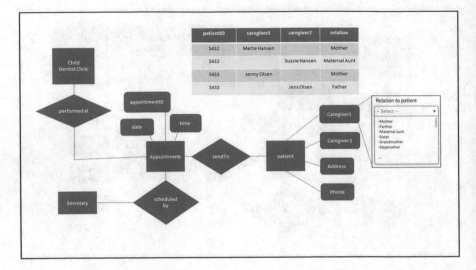

Fig. 7.2 Dental appointment database system, where 'mother' and 'father' are replaced by the category of 'caregiver'; illustration no. 2 of how the politics of classifications and categories is a technical problem

caregiver 2 in the database and potentially adding a dropdown menu to the user interface allowing the secretary to indicate the relation between child and caregiver.

Adding the 'relation' dropdown menu means implementing a new classification scheme for this technical design. It is evident that the classification scheme embedded in the dropdown menu for potential types of relations is based on certain assumptions about which relationships a pediatric dental patient can have. Such categories and classifications are based on assumptions embedded in society. In designing such a dropdown menu, the IT developer needs to consider the completeness of categories capturing a pediatric dental patient's relations. Such technical decisions thus require careful examination of the completeness of the classification, including that those dental patients might have two mothers or two fathers, or that patients in rainbow families have multiple fathers and mothers who together are responsible for the child's dental appointments.

Complicating the matter further in exploring the family structures in Denmark, it is not uncommon to have divorced families, where previous partners find new partners – and where families comprise 'mine', 'your', and 'our' children. Considering re-designing the pediatric dental appointment system based on the 2022 family structures in Denmark, we in Fig. 7.3 show how the database design with multiple relations between patients and caregivers could look like.

The database design in Fig. 7.3 is based on the fundamental assumption that patients can have one or more caregivers (1...*) and that each caregiver can have one or more relations to multiple patients (1...*). All schemes for classifying these relations have been removed from the database design. Instead, the algorithm for whom to inform about dental appointments is re-designed and is now based on a new

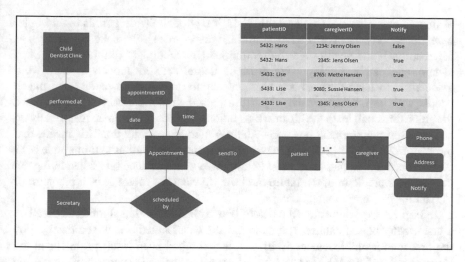

patientID	caregiverID	Notify
5432: Hans	1234: Jenny Olsen	false
5432: Hans	2345: Jens Olsen	true
5433: Lise	8765: Mette Hansen	true
5433: Lise	9080: Sussie Hansen	true
5433: Lise	2345: Jens Olsen	true

Fig. 7.3 Dental appointment database, where each child can have multiple caregivers and each caregiver can have multiple children, and where the algorithm is re-designed to use a Boolean notification feature (true/false) rather than the classification of caregiver; illustration no. 3 of how the politics of classifications and categories is a technical problem

variable, 'Notify', which is also included in the user interface, allowing the secretary to indicate whom to notify. This design imposes no limitations on different family structures, as the database 'table' in Fig. 7.3 demonstrates that Jenny Olsen and Jens Olsen have Hans as their child; when Hans has a dental appointment, Jens Olson need to be notified. Further, Lise is living with her mother, Mette Hansen, and her maternal aunt, Sussie Hansen, who both need to be notified of dental appointments. What we also see is that Jens Olson also has a relationship to Lise (his daughter from a previous marriage), and he also needs to be notified of dental appointments for Lise.

Our point here is not to provide a step-by-step introduction to database design but to demonstrate that each time an IT developer makes a technical decision and implements categories and classification systems, it matters for how the user interface, the algorithms, and the database structures are created and implemented. Decisions about database design structures matter for how to design appropriate algorithms which can search, relate, and manipulate the data. Decisions about algorithmic design matter for which kinds of data manipulations and visualizations can be produced to connect back to the database design. Finally, decisions on user interfaces also impact database design, since new features or variables implemented in the user interface need to be accommodated in the database structure. It is not enough to change, e.g., the gender classification scheme in a banking system from binary 'woman' and 'man' to include 'non-binary', 'other', and 'prefer not to say' if the fundamental statistics and visualizations continue to only report on binary data.

Clearly the above example is simplistic, and many IT systems are much more complex, embedding multiple and related databases which are not so easily examined and changed. One example is IT job portals. IT job portals often implement different types of predictive natural language processing technologies such as Microsoft's Word2vec to train the recommender functionality in the portal. Such technologies are trained by using different neural network models to learn word association in large datasets and uses the learned relations to predict and match people with jobs. When training algorithms based on historic data on job relations, the algorithms will learn the historic bias in jobs, such as that women historically do not hold top management positions whereas men historically do. This means that the historic bias will persist in newly implemented prediction systems unless IT developers and designers find ways to circumvent and balance bias considering not the past as a predictor of the future but how we want the future to be a predictor of the future.

In Fig. 7.4 we demonstrate the risk of bias embedded within algorithms based on a historically biased dataset. The example shows a LinkedIn message received by the first author on November 5, 2018, when she had been a full professor in the Department of Computer Science for 3 years. The message suggests that a top job pick was 'Easy Online Part-Time Job' as a 'Web Search Evaluator', which, if anyone should be in doubt, she was overqualified for. LinkedIn is not alone; several other recruitment tools at large IT companies such as Amazon have been trained to vet applications by learning patterns in historic resumes (Dastin 2018), clearly reintroducing bias from the past to the future.

Other large IT systems where the classification schemes and categories enable or constrain certain populations include IT systems for insurance, in immigration, in job centers, or in hospitals (Bjørn and Balka 2007; Boulus-Rødje 2018; Møller et al. 2019, 2021a, b; Asbjørn Ammitzbøll Flügge and Naja Holten Møller 2021; Petersen et al. 2021). For example, the classification schemes embedded in private insurance policies in Denmark have systematically let to mistreatment of pregnant women (Hall 2020). All insurance companies are highly digitalized in Denmark, which means that these policies have been enforced through IT systems, and thus that

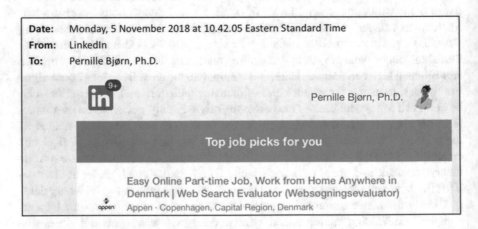

Fig. 7.4 Demonstrating bias in LinkedIn prediction of job

changing the behavior – following the law – requires re-designing the IT systems – databases, algorithms, and user interfaces.

As we showed above, the categories embedded in IT systems risk introducing problematic classification schemes which constrain certain populations. While this might not have been the IT developer's intention, it does not change the fact that when software designers, IT developers, and computer scientists – maybe unintentionally – design systems with problematic categories, it has real impacts on the lives of real people.

When computer scientists build a social media application for people to rent each other's homes (e.g., Airbnb) or develop a personal driving service where people drive others around in their own cars (e.g., Uber) (Sachs 2015; Kircher 2017), they use their own experiences of living and working in San Francisco's Silicon Valley as more generally applicable to other parts of the world. However, they tend to forget that the world is not the same everywhere, and that the conditions for travel or renting out houses vary.

To illustrate this point, let's look at an example from research conducted over several years by Nina Boulus-Rødje and the first author that explores challenges faced by tech entrepreneurs in Palestine. When we create technologies, these are socially situated within certain translocal infrastructures (Bjørn et al. 2017). You cannot import the technological concepts from Silicon Valley to Ramallah in the West Bank and expect success (Bjørn and Boulus-Rødje 2018). Tech entrepreneurs cannot simply adapt Western concepts to a land of occupation (Boulus-Rødje and Bjørn 2021). If the problem of getting parcels is not about local transportation and drop-off boxes but fundamentally about border control and harassment, there is no technological fix. Further, technology developed locally within Palestine cannot simply transcend the separation wall and reach the outside world (Boulus-Rødje et al. 2015; Boulus-Rødje and Bjørn 2019) if global technological infrastructures such as Apple's App Store or global payment gateways are inaccessible (Bjørn and Boulus-Rødje 2018).

Technology intersects with societal constructs such as workers' rights (Bødker et al. 1988; Kensing and Blomberg 1998) and through such encounters is transformed while transforming society. Tech entrepreneurs do not merely provide technological platforms allowing others to participate in the sharing economy. Instead, they risk unintentionally building an infrastructure that eliminates workers' rights (since they are not employees) and reinforces hidden structural racism in who gets to rent what kinds of houses (since landlords can choose tenants without justification) (Martin et al. 2014). For example, research found that prospective Airbnb guests with African American–sounding names are 16% less likely to be accepted than guests with White-sounding names (Edelman et al. 2017) and that facial recognition software does not work correctly on darker skin tones, introducing discrimination by design into Uber applications (Sachs 2015; Barry 2021).

Technologies have politics (Suchman 2003) – intentional as well as unintentional – and it is urgently important that we train new computer scientists to take their share of the responsibility for identifying and taking actions to reduce the risks of constraints for certain users embedded in the design. If problematic classifications are embedded in technology producing biased interfaces, biased database systems, or biased algorithms, it is vital that technology developers be trained to analyze and discover such problems – allowing them to correct the problems or perhaps prevent them in the first place.

A good way to begin is to ensure a diverse workforce: a diverse group of tech developers and designers. This agenda is increasingly gaining traction in the industry and in education. But we also need to educate and empower tech developers, including computer scientists, to prevent the creation of bias and barriers that can act as exclusion mechanisms. Positive change needs to be embraced at multiple levels in the computing ecosystem, besides the mere introduction of "diverse" teams. We argue for the need to introduce structural changes in both tech education and the tech industry. Such changes take time and effort, and we suggest beginning with including critical approaches to computing and accessibility into the core computer science curriculum, as researchers in computing education have been increasingly advocating for (Ko et al. 2020). Further we must ensure that organizations do not just engage in what former Google researcher Timnit Gebru referred to in an interview as "diversity theatre" (Preston 2021), when diversity commitments fail to truly empower and support the work of (often under-represented social groups) in the areas of bias prevention and equity.

Note that the implied user is often built in the image of the designer or developer, since people act and develop based on what they know and experience. However, users of technology are multiple and diverse simultaneously; if you develop a technology for a pharmacy in Danish society, you might have homogeneity across pharmacies. However, while each pharmacy generally follows the same procedures, contextual contingencies will always exist and must be considered in technology design (Bjørn et al. 2009). Thus, if we move the pharmacy technology to the Philippines, the main purpose of the pharmacy remains the same, but the procedures might differ vastly, resulting in different use of language and vocabulary within the IT system (Jensen and Bjørn 2012). Developing technology for the global market clearly requires us to work in teams with diverse perspectives and backgrounds to ensure that we consider the potential barriers that we risk building into our systems, allowing us to take steps to make them more inclusive – or at least not exclusive by design (Møller et al. 2017; Møller 2018; Matthiesen et al. 2020, 2022).

The FemTech agenda sees the responsibility for addressing the risk of embedded bias in system design as collective: empowering change begins in education, within computer science programs, enabling graduating computer scientists to think critically and intentionally about the power of classification schemes and the impact of bias built into technologies, and thus to make better choices when designing and maintaining digital interfaces and infrastructures.

Diversity Dimensions and Equity Classification

Studying equity and inclusion in computer science from an interventionist perspective provides different challenges and opportunities for our endeavors. Our role as insiders (being computer scientists) meant that we had prior relevant knowledge about practices (e.g., programming), vocabulary (e.g., nerd culture), and artefacts (e.g., micro-processors). However, from ethnographic approaches, we must acknowledge that being an insider does not make you an expert in studying your own field (Forsythe 1993, 1999, 2001). Basic assumptions about the field risk hiding important aspects that need scrutinizing. Important aspects of the practices risk being invisible to insiders, who simply take such aspects for granted rather than question their very existence through examination. Further, as researchers, we knew that important knowledge about gender, equity, and inclusion already existed in research literature. Thus, as with any other new domain, we needed to become familiar with the core concepts and research vocabulary – not just within the field of computer science (empirical focus) but also within existing research on gender and equity (theoretical focus). We needed theoretical concepts to help us question fundamental assumptions within the empirical field to make them noticeable and visibly available for scrutinizing. Thus, an important part of FemTech research is to establish a theoretical reasoning that can help us explore our own blind spots as insiders in the field.

In this section we want the reader to reflect on how social inequalities in tech manifest in relation to specific social markers – we call this a *diversity classification scheme*. The scheme is not exhaustive, and it is meant to be open; each context would call for additional dimensions. We also want the reader to reflect on the different areas in which social inequalities in technology can manifest. A diversity classification scheme is not only about gender but fundamentally about all different kinds of ways that people can be unique while still being part of a larger community – and the different ways in which social inequality can manifest in relation to these differences such as sexism, racism, and ableism, just to name a few. A diversity classification scheme is not a checklist but an incomplete list of aspects that technology designers and developers need to consider and critically reflect on to understand how the dynamics of social inequalities manifest in relation to forms of human diversity shaped by technology.

There are four main areas where social inequalities can manifest in technology design and development: (1) user interfaces, (2) databases & data structure, (3) algorithms, and (4) team composition & power dynamics. The first three areas concern the technical design and link back to the prior section: "Technologies have embedded politics and it's a technical problem", where we unpack how diversity and equity is a technical problem. The risk of social inequality embedded in user interface design, database design, and algorithms often considers 'an omnipotent user' stripped of all social markers for the design. However, the world is full of diverse people, and when engaging with biased technology, people 'who do not fit the characteristics of the omnipotent user' will be constrained in their interactions

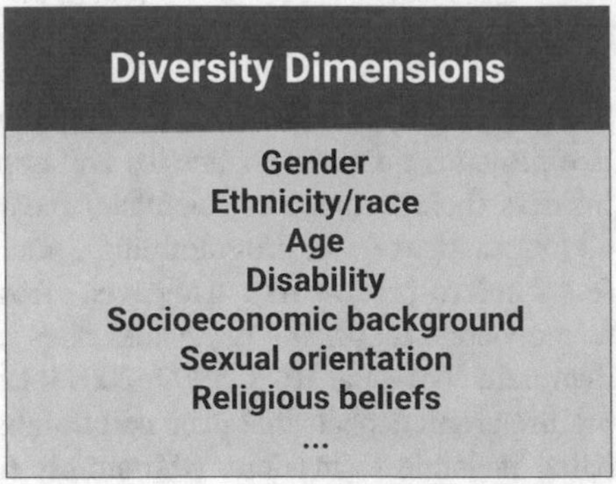

Fig. 7.5 Diversity
dimensions & social
identifies – an
incomplete list

Diversity Dimensions
Gender Ethnicity/race Age Disability Socioeconomic background Sexual orientation Religious beliefs ...

with the technology. The fourth area is then related to the actual design and development process of technology, considering 'who' belongs to the group of people developing technologies as well as the hierarchy, decision power, and power dynamics. All four areas are important if we want to create unique, innovative, and relevant technologies and be mindful of bias and how biases can manifest in technologies, along different social markers – in the design, testing, maintenance, and use of technology. The diversity classification scheme is relevant for all four areas.

Fundamentally, there are infinite diversity dimensions that are relevant for technology design – including gender, race/ethnicity, disability, age, sexuality, religion, and socioeconomic background – depending on which kinds of individual projects and technologies are being designed. Technologies are used by everyone; thus, technologies should be able to express and consider all kinds of diversity dimensions (Fig. 7.5).

Gender as a diversity dimension for technology has broadly received much attention within computer science research in the last couple of years (Breslin and Wadhwa 2014; Hicks 2017; Buolamwini and Gebru 2018; Frieze and Quesenberry 2019; D'Ignazio and Klein 2020; Albusays et al. 2021). When we created FemTech in 2016, a gender lens was our focus and has guided much of our work throughout all the design artefacts presented in this book. We originally conformed to a cisgender binary framework, influenced by our institution's focus on "attracting more women" to computing, rather than being intentionally inclusive of trans*, intersex, and gender-non-conforming people. In current editions, we ensure that expansive gender language is used, intentionally targeting people from all under-represented gender identities. However, from the beginning we strived to create not gendered artefacts but artefacts that were as gender-neutral as possible. We were not successful in this with Cyberbear, but we did succeed in this with GRACE and Cryptosphere.

Moving forward with initiatives, events, and strategies, we consider gender as a non-binary dimension that includes trans* and other gender-non-conforming identities. Gender is a social construct, shaped by social norms, and different societies have different gender norms that again affect people differently. Since our work focuses on gender diversity in computing in a Scandinavian country, these are the gender norms we engaged in our design artefacts. However, we are well aware that different gender norms exist, and that other initiatives in other countries should identify, address, and challenge the gender norms shaping computer science in those countries.

Ethnicity/race as a diversity dimension for technology was put on the agenda in 2020 with the increased mobilization of the Black Lives Matter movement in the USA and in human computer interaction research (Ogbonnaya-Ogburu et al. 2020). Understanding ethnicity and race from a global perspective is difficult. The concept of race is foundational to systemic repression in, for example, the USA (Noble 2018), and racial classifications are social constructions first and foremost developed and performed through historic situations of slavery and colonization (Benjamin 2019a, b). Racial and ethnic classifications are constructed differently in different contexts, and social inequalities that manifest in relation to them are unfortunately pervasive: technology is increasingly scrutinized as one of the areas in which racism and discrimination are embedded, with harmful social impacts. Racism also exists in Scandinavia, including Denmark. Thus, it is important for the design of technologies to consider the ways in which ethnicity produces social inequality to ensure that problematic societal markers are not being reproduced and potentially re-enforced through IT system designs. Ethnicity is an important diversity dimension to include in equity interventions and needs to be situated within the specific societal context considered for a technology design.

Being honest about our own work, we initially in 2016 did not address ethnicity as a diversity dimension explicitly in our design artefacts; however, we did have a strong focus on including participants from a wide range of socioeconomic backgrounds, and we focused on reaching out to non-Danes, ensuring that all our events were in English. When we recruited participants for the FemTech workshops, we initially explicitly reached out to high schools in the lower socioeconomic areas of Copenhagen, which also provided us a diverse group of participants in terms of ethnicity.

Age as a diversity dimension for technology includes considerations for how to address various aspects of the growing elderly population for technology design (Tellioğlu et al. 2014; Hornung et al. 2017) as well as for children and youth (Boyd 2007; Thyssen 2015; Pinkard et al. 2017). We need to consider the digital divide between digital natives growing up with the internet and having different advantages for technology use and older adults for whom internet access is not necessarily a main part of their lives. Age in technology development is also related to privacy and security, such as considerations of who has access to which types of data under which conditions (e.g., parents' access to children's data) and of when people are considered adults, which varies between societies. Age can also be considered in terms of experience, as a number, or in terms of bodily decay. How we understand age depends on the living conditions of a specific geographical location. We have not directly addressed age in our design of artefacts and events. However, while most participants in our FemTech workshops were teenagers, a few were in their twenties. These were people who for different reasons had moved to Denmark from abroad (as refugees or immigrants) and thus began high school later. At the GRACE events, we had mixed age groups; at the Danish event, participants ranged from primary school children to retirees. At the two conference events, we estimated the participants to be 22–60 years old.

Disability as a diversity dimension for technology includes considerations of both mental and physical health. Disability studies in computer science is an ongoing attempt to include voices related to personal and social experiences of disability in the academic field (Spiel et al. 2020). Mental and physical health can shape people's experiences and access to technologies (e.g., blind software developers use screen readers for programming (Potluri et al. 2018)). However, instead of viewing disability as primarily the loss of a function in an individual (the so-called medical model of disability), contemporary research stresses how disability arises in the interaction between functional limitations and impairments and social and physical barriers (social model of disability). Disability is used also as an analytical lens to identify problems that can be a vehicle for developing new areas for research. As stated by Jennifer Mankoff, Gillian Hayes, and Devva Kasnitz: *"A better understanding of what constitutes a problem from a disability studies perspective can help to enrich existing research and illuminate new areas of inquiry"* (Mankoff et al. 2010, p. 3). Thus, critically addressing and understanding how people with a disability (temporary, permanent, or situational) face barriers in sociotechnical spaces also offers an opportunity to drive the field of technology design forward for all. In FemTech, we have not addressed disability in our published work, but current FemTech work by the third author of this book is pushing the agenda further, considering how we can bring in disability and accessibility as part of FemTech.

Socioeconomic background as a diversity dimension for technology places the focus on the socioeconomic backgrounds of people and places, and how such aspects shape people's access to or inaccessibility to engage with technology. Often technology is articulated as the driver of making the world equally accessible to everybody – and how, for example, digital platforms remove physical borders in a globalized world. However, barriers remain. Classist algorithms using healthcare spending as a proxy for healthcare needs or using collected health data on wearable devices to determine health insurance costs perpetuate inequalities (Christophersen et al. 2015; Vartan 2019). Bias manifesting along nationalities and geographical contexts, rooted in colonialism, are still prevalent. There are distinct differences between working as a software developer in the Global South versus the Global North (Bjørn 2019). Where you are located matters for your translocal contingencies (Bjørn et al. 2017), infrastructural accessibility (Bjørn and Boulus-Rødje 2018), or implicit bias (Matthiesen et al. 2022) and shapes the global encounters mediated by technology in different ways. By paying attention to socioeconomic and geopolitical conditions (e.g., for refugees (Stickel et al. 2015)), when we explore and design technology, we will notice the nature of the taken-for-granted assumptions about sociotechnical infrastructures that serve as the foundation for contemporary technology development. This will allow us to challenge the status quo and begin creating inclusive and diverse technology development practices, which are accessible for a larger global group.

Sexual orientation and religious beliefs are diversity dimensions relevant for technology in considering both the classification schemes we embed in the applications (Abid et al. 2021) and how people's personal beliefs or sexual orientation are important areas for technology innovation (Mustafa et al. 2020). As with other diversity dimensions, sexual orientation and religious beliefs open the design space for technology development. Muslim prayer practices were the driving force for adding a digital compass to smartphones, now standard in most phones; and dating apps are examples of the importance of diversity in sexual orientation and religious beliefs for the analytical design perspectives of technology (Hariri et al. 2021). However, additional considerations are important. In the rise of social media, we have also witnessed a new type of situation where sexual orientation and religious beliefs have driven online harassment in anonymous fora (Rubin et al. 2020) and in the workplace (Tenorio and Bjørn 2019) (Fig. 7.5).

As we work to create inclusive environments, we need to consider the different diversity dimensions and acknowledge that diversity is not always something you can 'see'. You cannot immediately see who people are, where they come from, or which 'characteristics' contribute to making them who they are. In creating an inclusive environment, whether for computer science education, software development work, or any other aspect of society where digital technologies are used, we must consider that people are different and assume that the people we design for are different from ourselves. We cannot rely on our own experiences and bodies as a template for others. The unconscious process by which designers configure users as fundamentally resembling themselves is defined as "I-methodology" (Akrich 1995), and this implicit representation process presents clear constraints even for user-centered design practices (Oudshoorn et al. 2004). Software developers and designers must learn as part of their education to be mindful and aware of the biases that can occur in design processes and in the application of technology to different sociocultural contexts. Being aware of the multiple intersecting diversity dimensions, and of how they can affect the design of interfaces, databases, and algorithms, is necessary to actively get an edge in our digital innovations. By designing while keeping in mind the rich variety of social identities, we improve technology for all people instead of just a few (who typically resemble the individuals who make up technology design teams). In having a diverse and inclusive workplace that considers the rich variety of human difference and that is mindful of the social dynamics that manifest in relation to diversity, we have direct access to noticing and identifying the otherwise invisible exclusive mechanisms in our technologies – which can give tech companies a competitive advantage over other software company competitors. Software developers and computer scientists in their education will benefit greatly from learning about and experiencing working actively with diversity dimensions, connected social identities, and related mechanisms of bias and discrimination, enabling them to use these insights when developing digital technologies. It has always been fundamental to computer science education and software development practice to work together in teams and with people from different professions. When designing IT system for pharmacies, software developers need to be able to talk with pharmacists, and when designing IT systems for healthcare practitioners, they need to be able to talk to doctors and nurses. Thus, the skills required to engage with other professions with the aim of designing technologies are part of the core curriculum of computer science. Collaborating and communicating are fundamental skills and expertise that are critically important to designing technology for people and society.

We argue in this book for extending the existing perspective on user-centered design and including teaching and learning about diversity dimensions in technology development as core and fundamental skills and expertise for two reasons. First, because paying attention to diversity dimensions connected to social identities opens the field of computer science in terms of who belongs and can succeed in the field; second, because diversity dimensions can be used strategically in technology design to reveal spaces for new innovations, technologies, and practices shaping a just and fair society of tomorrow.

Equity and Intersectionality

The diversity dimensions introduced above are important as individual dimensions, and together they benefit technology research and innovation by extending the analytical and design agendas in novel directions. However, rather than use these dimensions as a mere checklist for innovation, we must pay attention to the historic conditions that created unbalanced participation in the first place. The dynamics of social inequality have historically manifested in relation to social identities (gender, race/ethnicity, age, etc.), having a concrete impact on the starting point for individuals' actions. We must consider the history that produced certain unequal situations in society in general to understand the unbalanced diversity in computer science. "[E]qual process (…) make[s] no sense at all in a society in which identifiable groups had actually been treated differently historically and in which the effects of this difference in treatment continued into the present" (Crenshaw 1988, p. 1345). Different societies have different historical backgrounds; thus, comprehending how the different diversity dimensions are shaped historically requires insights into the historically situated conditions. The practice of ensuring diversity and inclusion is not a process of equal access for all, since the conditions for people to participate at the outset are not equal.

Moving into the situated historical conditions for computer science in Denmark, introduced in the beginning of this book, we need to pay attention to social inequality as it manifests in the field, indicated by the numbers of women and other gender-minority faculty in the computer science department; the so-called Matthaeus effect for distributing grants, indicating a self-reinforcing mechanism whereby already successful researchers keep getting funded; and the statistics for the privilege of supervising PhD students (see Chap. 1). While some women have succeeded as computer scientists and received national and international recognition, only very recently (since 2016) can we detect an improvement in numbers in Denmark. To understand the current situation, we need to revisit the history of computer science.

Historically, computer science as a field and domain emerged during WWII, as men historically were recruited to the military as soldiers while women worked on measuring missile trajectories or breaking communication codes (Ensmenger 2010;

Hicks 2017). The term "software engineering" was coined by a woman, Margaret Hamilton, and the first computer bug was found by another woman, Grace Hopper. Katherine Johnson, Dorothy Vaughn, and Mary Jackson worked at NASA as 'computers', where they made the calculations allowing for space travel. Software was woven by threaded copper wires into the core rope memory for the Apollo moon landing by women working as Raytheon's expert seamstresses, nicknamed 'Little Old Ladies' (Rosner et al. 2018a, b). The ENIAC women were the first to program a general purpose computer (Ensmenger 2010), and Jean Valentine, Joan Clarke, Margaret Rock, Mavis Lever, and Ruth Briggs all worked to break Nazi Germany's Enigma code at Bletchley Park. Computer science and programming began as a women's occupation in the USA and UK.

During WWII, Denmark was occupied by Germany and thus was not part of developing the field of computing via military endeavors. This meant that computing did not arrive in Denmark until after the war, and here computing began in industry (Sveinsdottir and Frøkjær 1988). We know little about the work of the early women in the Danish computing industry, since it is not well documented; however, in a few places women are mentioned as 'hulkort damer' (punch-card ladies). When computer science became an academic field in 1970, it was during the student rebellion in which universities in Denmark changed from being controlled by professors (the vast majority being men) to allow equal representation for student and staff on different committees. There were women when computer science was first created; however, only one woman, Edda Sveinsdottir, is mentioned by name in the written history (DIKU 2021). There are no gender statistics available from the University of Copenhagen until 1997; however, that year there were 18 women out of 241 students (7.47%). The years with the lowest numbers of women students were 2004 (3.66%) and 2011 (3.9%), when their share was below 4% (Forskningsministeriet 2021). These low percentages are surprising given that Denmark is known for its high ranking for equality; however, in recent years Denmark has not been among the top 10 countries on the equality index, and even our Nordic neighbors Iceland, Norway, Finland, and Sweden occupy the top 4 positions (Forum 2020).

Birgitte Possing, a professor of history and women in Denmark, tries in her book to unpack some of the conditions explaining historical gender inequality in Denmark (Possing 2018). Referring to professor of law Hanne Petersen, she suggests that in the '80s and '90s there was a marriage between two different political movements in Denmark. On one hand was the historical embedded cooperative movement ("andelstanken") stipulating that all are equal, and which has been strong in Denmark since the 1700s. On the other hand, a new liberal thinking was introduced in the late '90s, often referred to by the slogan "du er din egen lykkes smed", which can be understood as a Danish version of the American "dream", meaning that you are responsible for your own success and that if you fail, it's your own fault. Thus, responsibility for equal conditions in Denmark was left to the individual, and formal organizations responsible for ensuring equality were shut down in 2000 (Possing 2018). Possing proposes that one explanation for Denmark's lack of gender equity is that when society combines the cooperative idea that everybody is equal with that of individual responsibility for ensuring equal access, any analysis of or pointing to problematical existing structures with unequal conditions becomes an individual concern rather than a collective responsibility.

The very idea and understanding that there are fundamental conditions embedded in society causing some people to have privilege and better conditions for success than others – and that these conditions are based on people's gender, ethnicity, disability, or socioeconomic conditions – must be acknowledged as the starting point before new initiatives to make change can have long-term impact.

Following Possing's argument, as part of a process towards making computer science diverse and inclusive, we must consider the historically unequal conditions in academia based on gender, ethnicity, disability, or socioeconomic background. We need to pay attention to the people who are under- or unrepresented within the field and find ways to mobilize and encourage their efforts in joining and using the opportunities that digital skills and expertise bring for social mobility in the society. We must find ways to allow under-represented groups in computer science to enter and shape the field in their own ways, creating new agendas for technology design and use. It is not about getting people who are currently not included to fit into existing schemes stipulating the nature of computer science and computer scientists. Instead, the approach we argue for in this book is to open the field and allow newcomers from diverse backgrounds to shape and transform the field to their interests and perspectives, and to recognize that we all have responsibility for collective, structural change in order to empower new perspectives and new efforts that push against normative frameworks. Encouraging diversity in computer science is *not about equality, it is about equity*.

Equity is a concern directed at balancing the support, encouragement, cost, and so on, in relation to the benefit, reward, outcome, et cetera, of an activity, taking into account individual conditions. Thus, equity is fundamentally about the fair distribution of resources based on actual need, which requires us to be better equipped to critically assess whose needs have been overlooked and which groups are more likely to incur negative social outcomes due to bias and discrimination. This means that making change is not about providing equal opportunity for all but about identifying who is excluded and focusing our interventions there. Further, making interventions towards equity is not an individual responsibility but a collective responsibility directed at providing and improving the conditions for equity.

So, what does collective group responsibility really mean? Ogbonnaya-Ogburu, Smith, To, and Toyama provide an excellent example of this in their 2020 paper on critical race theory (Ogbonnaya-Ogburu et al. 2020). They list an immediate estimation of the 133 CHI Academy – a prestigious award and recognition in the research field of human–computer interaction – showing that more than 90% recipients were White and that none were of Black/African descent (ibid.). The CHI Academy is supposed to be global and thus has a collective responsibility to ensure that people recognized within the field represent the community. Celebrating people's achievements is a collective responsibility of the field, and we as researchers should carefully consider whether we are considering all relevant people or whether we are unintentionally neglecting and overlooking people who do not fit the norm. Being chosen for such an honor is not an objective decision but always a negotiation among groups with people of power (who have already been chosen earlier); thus, groups in power need to consider their own privilege and provide space (and power) to others if we are to see a change. Equity is about providing space, privilege, and power to people entering and transforming the field in new ways – people who are not the norm but who will take the field in new and innovative directions. In such efforts it is critical that we consider that the *diversity dimensions intersect*. Where diversity dimensions intersect, active attention is required to reduce the risk of neglecting important achievements (since they do not fit the norm of evaluating achievement) and recognize how individual conditions serve as barriers.

Intersectionality refers to the complex overlapping of diversity dimensions, created to consider the problematic consequences of treating race and gender as mutually exclusive categories of experience and analysis (Crenshaw 1989, p. 139). The problem is that we tend to consider one category exclusively rather than how the categories interlink. "Women" tends to mean White women, and "Black" tends to mean Black men. In her famous paper, Kimberlé Crenshaw shows how a Black woman failed in her legal efforts to demonstrate that General Motors did not hire Black women before 1964 and fired all Black women hired after 1970. General Motors successfully argued that they hired women (White) as well as Black (men) and thus she could not show discrimination since some parts of the case focused on race and others on gender – and that these dimensions were seen as mutually exclusive categories (Crenshaw 1989). Exploring the experiences of Black women in computing, Ranking and Thomas find that "because women of color share the same gender as white women but differ in race, they are subjugated to a different reality and set of social injustices that are often ignored by gender-focused efforts" (Rankin and Thomas 2020, p. 199).

It is critically important to consider how the diversity dimensions intersect instead of addressing categories as mutually exclusive; focusing on single categories means that certain populations risk falling between them and thus are neglected in interventions. They end up as residual categories (Matthiesen and Bjørn 2016, 2017; Matthiesen et al. 2020, 2022) in our diversity dimension classification. Residual categories are the "in-between" categories that do not fit the formal classifications because they are neither-nor. When aspects, things, people, concepts, identities, and so forth are residual, they risk being overlooked and becoming invisible. They do not exist as part of the society receiving attention and thus are forgotten and potentially unintentionally omitted from technology design considerations. Stina Matthiesen in her research on global software development shows how the classification schemes of corporate email addresses disadvantaged software developers working from Poland compared with software developers working from Denmark (Matthiesen et al. 2020). As it turned out, an international company assigned email addresses to developers in Denmark using abbreviations of people's names; however, software developers in Poland were assigned email addresses beginning with 'xxx', indicating that they were not physically located in Denmark. Their colleagues would not respond promptly to emails from addresses beginning with 'xxx' because this classification was also used for external consultants, who were not seen as part of the company, and thus not important to answer rapidly.

Because of this labeling and classification scheme, software developers working outside Denmark were disproportionally ignored. This was due not to gender, socio-economic, ability, or other individual diversity dimensions but to the intersection between perspectives on external consultants and perspectives on global work.

Cultural Taxation and the Imposter Phenomenon

Reaching for equity for all – considering all the diversity dimensions – is a direction and future goal, not where computer science and software development are in 2022. To make the change, we need multiple people from around the globe and in different professions and research areas of computer science education and practice to pave the road to equity and inclusion. Responsibility for gender diversity should not uniquely fall to women and gender minorities to advocate, and it is not the responsibility of immigrants to advocate for ethnic diversity. Instead, it is the work of the majority and of people with power in the field to notice and create space to invite and distribute power for otherwise invisible voices. Equity is also a process of decision power, and of how new groups need to get voice and access to the distribution of value. What counts as value depends on the context – in academia, value includes things like citations, awards, grants, and mentoring of PhD students – and all these criteria are mutually dependent (see Chap. 1). What is often not valued is the effort involved in equity work.

Equity work takes effort and resources and often adds extra work of advocacy for under-represented groups. Often institutions seeking to attract more people from diverse backgrounds will ask the few people within under-represented groups to act as mentors, as role models, and to be visible – atop existing advocacy work and their normal work. Concretely, we, the authors of this book, have multiple times joined events internal or external to the university with the purpose of recruiting more women to computer science. We have been asked to recruit current computer science students from our own program, to help others by acting as mentors or as instructors for programming workshops for women and non-binary individuals. While good intentions underlie these invitations, such work is often unpaid, takes time away from work on subject matter (students' studies or our research), and is not valued as real work. Fundamentally, such efforts – while important – do not add to people's CVs more than a little 'nice to have', so while peers from majority groups do not have to join such activities, they simply have more time to focus on their individual carriers or studies. The extra burden of diversity work thus risks reducing under-represented groups' opportunities for individual success. This extra work of minority groups has been identified as *cultural taxation* by Amada Padilla (Padilla 1994; Joseph and Hirshfield 2011).

Cultural taxation is the "obligation to show good citizenship towards the institution by serving its needs for ethnic representation on committees, or to demonstrate knowledge and commitment to a cultural group, which may even bring accolades to the institution but which is not usually rewarded by the institution on whose behalf the service is performed" (Padilla 1994, p. 26). The problem here is not whether diversity work is important for the institution: it is. The problem is that diversity work is seen as important but that, in terms of reward systems for promotion, graduating with excellence, or receiving awards, it is not viewed as relevant for estimating intellectual excellence. Thus, each time under-represented groups spend time and effort on diversity work, they risk reducing the quality of their own resumes. Further, organizations often fail to understand and acknowledge that diversity work cannot simply be turned on and off but is instead embedded in the lived experiences and interactions of under-represented individuals, which at times can be extremely stressful and pose a high risk of burnout (Padilla 1994). Visibility of diverse representation is important – under-represented groups benefit from 'seeing' themselves represented in faculty and in auditoriums, and their opinions are important for decision-making. However, it is an ongoing challenge for organizations to ensure that under-represented groups spend their limited time and representation on important and impactful agendas while supporting their careers. Further, organizations should consider how to appreciate the value of diversity work as part of excellence with direct link to awards, promotions, prestige, and privilege. Diversity work of under-presented groups is needed to push the balance towards equity, and seeing under-represented groups succeed is critical for the experience of belonging to a field.

The term *imposter phenomenon* has been used to describe the feeling of not belonging to a field, profession, or community despite results, qualifications, and competences (Clance and Imes 1978). This phenomenon (also referred to as the imposter syndrome) has particularly been identified in high-achievement environments of high competition such as academia (Langford and Clance 1993). Studies have shown that the imposter phenomenon is more prevalent in women and members of under-represented racial, ethnic, and religious groups; thus, researchers have argued that organizations must pay attention to these challenges, which risk countering diversity efforts (Chrousos and Mentis 2020). Actions to mitigate the imposter experience have been proposed as therapeutic approaches; the former chief operating officer at Facebook Sheryl Sandberg wrote the controversial book *Lean In*, wherein she proposes that women overcome the imposter syndrome and take leadership by *leaning in* and sitting at the table (Sandberg 2013). While we do not doubt the presence of the imposter phenomenon in high-achievement environments, we would argue that by introducing the imposter syndrome to the discussion on equity, we risk moving responsibility for the alien experience of under-represented groups from the external surroundings to a personal internalization. Sandberg, in her guidebook for women in tech leadership, places the responsibility for women's success on women's own abilities and performance – hiding the role of the institutional conditions that produce unbalanced access to success. The fundamental message in *Lean In* is that women must themselves take power – it is not given to them. However, the missing message is that people in power must relinquish some of their power if organizations are to provide space for alternative voices. Navigating the imposter syndrome – which fundamentally is about discomfort and anxiety in high-achievement workplaces – is not about teaching under-represented groups more technical skills and expertise while allowing them to navigate in existing biased organizational situations. Instead, it is about changing structurally biased circumstances, allowing them to succeed on their own terms and develop themselves as well as the field of digital technology. In the words of Ruchikan Tulshyan and Jodi-Ann Burey, "Stop telling women they have imposter syndrome"; we should be "fixing bias, not women" (Tulshyan and Burey 2021). It is critically important that we not place the responsibility on the individual to join in but instead consider this challenge of equity as a collective responsibility we all must take – especially people in power.

Equity initiatives are not about creating diversity committees – populated by under-represented groups paying cultural taxes – who can then advise and council decision-makers. Instead, equity initiatives are about inviting the under-represented groups to be full members of the decision power committees and ensuring that the interaction and communication – language and vocabulary – are appropriate for diverse groups and having a respectful and genuine interest in making a change. Women like Sheryl Sandberg who have reached top positions are not automatically the best advocates for equity, since they have managed to navigate the current circumstances and, in that process, risk internalizing the systemic bias on which the system is built. In the process of becoming successful, the few under-represented individuals do much work to fit in and internalize the same metrics and behaviors for what success entails. Therefore, when inviting under-represented individuals to join important decisions as full members, it is important to consider (1) how we can recruit and invite people with different perspectives from ours, and (2) how we can train all decision-makers in equity as a collective responsibility. We cannot expect that simply because an individual is from an under-represented group they are interested in building or know how to build an organization characterized by equity. The challenge for decision-makers (no matter their background) is to figure out how to mainstream equity within the organization.

Chapter 8
Organizational Change for Equity & Inclusion

In this chapter, we situate how the insights in equity and inclusion we have gained through the FemTech research can inform how organizations such as computer science departments or tech companies can step up and improve inclusivity. We cannot offer a complete set of guidelines, but we can propose agendas, questions, and considerations which hopefully can assist organizations in creating their own strategies for intervention.

First, it is important to state that increasing diversity and reducing homogeneity related to gender in computer science organizations will not benefit from an essentialist focus on cis- and binary gender differences. No relevant insights will come from using specific stereotypical characteristics of, for example, women and men related to computer science as a lens through which to make a change. Women and men are not two exclusive categories possessing certain characteristics related to technology, computer science, or programming. It is not more difficult for women to learn how to program, and plenty of excellent women are very technically inclined and extraordinary programmers. Similarly, some men have no prior experience in programming when entering a bachelor's-level program in computer science and struggle to get through. Just to be clear: women do not have specific characteristics that make it more difficult for them than men to work with computer science topics, methods, or domains.

> We propose that organizations, instead of considering the unbalanced gender statistics as the central problem to solve, will benefit from considering the statistics as a symptom of how systemic structures, traditions, and culture within the organizations privilege and award certain kind of behaviors and interactions while constraining others.

© The Author(s) 2023
P. Bjørn et al., *Diversity in Computer Science*,
https://doi.org/10.1007/978-3-031-13314-5_8

Empowering People Considering Multiple Diversity Dimensions

The main problem is not the innate inability of specific social groups to engage with tech design and development (as some prejudiced views still hold) but rather the existence of inequitable conditions for true access to the tech playing field that derive from a combination of factors that are more or less relevant in different social contexts: exclusionary cultures in computing, ableist infrastructures, digital divides, preparatory privilege (indicating the many extra-curricular courses and activities mostly engaging boys, for instance), and social norms linking choices of tech careers and even the existence of tech skills to specific genders, cultures, and ethnicities. It is vital that we expend effort and resources to allow equitable access to and conditions of computer science, which sometimes includes programming workshops designed for certain populations.

Improving and finding new ways to teach programming for all is critical. Jane Margolis and Allan Fisher document that before interventions that led to 50/50 gender diversity, the computer science curriculum and teaching structures at Carnegie Mellon University were hurting all students, and that these structures particularly served as a barrier for women and under-presented groups who felt vulnerable in an unfamiliar territory when they began their education. For example, large courses trying to teach too broad a range of students made "students who are less experienced feel that the professors assume students know more than they do" (Margolis and Fisher 2003, p. 83), since they experienced their peers describing the curriculum as 'easy', 'boring', and 'repetitive', while they themselves were 'drowning' (ibid.). Similarly, reporting from the experiences from Harvey Mudd College, Alvarado and Libeskind-Hadas (2012) found that large classes with students spanning a wide range of experience in programming upon entering a program was identified as a barrier. This insight led the institution to create two parallel initial computer science courses (Gold: 'no prior experience in programming'; and Black, 'prior experience in programming'), which both led to the same second computer science course in the next semester (Alvarado et al. 2012). The 'outsider-ness' experienced by underrepresented groups in computer science made the students much more vulnerable to problematic teaching environments, which led them to leave the field even in an otherwise welcoming environment (Margolis and Fisher 2003). It is not our agenda here to discuss how to best teach computer science; instead, we aim here to encourage organizations to remember that time spent improving the conditions for underrepresented groups is fundamentally about improving the conditions for all.

Improving conditions for under-represented groups in computer science organizations includes considering all the diversity dimensions and their intersections (see Chap. 7). Meredith Ringel Morris, Andrew Begel, and Ben Wiedermann studied the challenges of neurodiverse software engineering employees at Microsoft and found that a major challenge was working in noisy environments (Morris et al. 2015). Software engineers working in open offices is not uncommon; however, this office layout might compromise the efficiency of neurodiverse software developers. From an intersectionality perspective (Crenshaw 1989), combining gender and cognitive abilities (gender and disability diversity dimensions), women software engineers diagnosed with neurodiversity risk being *disproportionally* harmed by noisy work environments as well as educational structures of large classes. Research on open office spaces shows that such designs are negatively related to employee satisfaction and productivity (Brennan et al. 2002). Thus, by accommodating software engineers with neurodiversity in terms of office layout, we also improve teaching environments for neurotypical software engineers.

> We propose that organizations take a multi-dimensional perspective on diversity including, but not limited to, gender, ethnicity, disability, age, socioeconomic background, and so forth, and that they consider the ways in which infrastructures, including physical layouts, technological platforms, and work processes, enable or constrain a diverse group and take action to accommodate an inclusive environment.

Diversifying Computer Science Stereotypes

Working explicitly with diversifying tech organizations (education and IT industry) benefits from breaking down existing narrowly defined stereotypes within and outside formal and informal spaces. Historically, computer science began as female (Hicks 2017); yet, over time, the prevalent computer science stereotype became masculine, celebrating the male subculture of computer hacking (Ensmenger 2010). Nathan Ensmenger (2010) documents how this change was accidental but continues to be reinforced and institutionalized today. Ensmenger points out that the stereotypical notion of "the antisocial programmer, wearing sandals and a beard" was a deliberate self-construction rather than emerging from the initial field of computing (Ensmenger 2010, p. 240), a stereotype repeated in public culture such as in popular TV series like *Silicon Valley*, *The IT Crowd*, and *The Big Bang Theory*.

A crucial part of becoming an inclusive organization is breaking with the singular stereotype of the computer scientist as a male geek and instead opening up to alternative definitions of computer scientist (Frieze and Quesenberry 2013, 2015). It is important to challenge stereotypes and to extend and multiply narratives about who can belong to and succeed in the field. The emergence of new co-existing and parallel alternative narratives about who belongs in computer science is profoundly important for the field's long-term transformation. It is about developing the organization professionally. The organization must be developed in tandem with institutional support for and a professional organization of inclusive initiatives driving the change for diversity while improving the organization for all (Frieze and Quesenberry 2015, p. 77). Diversity initiatives should not only be about outreach and communication or about organizing yearly recruiting events or celebrating Ada Lovelace Day and International Women's Day. Diversity initiatives are not about changing members of other under-represented groups to make them fit into existing structures. Instead, the diversity, inclusion, and equity agenda is about re-thinking institutional structures, including language and symbolic representations, events, norms, and artefacts embedded in certain cultural perceptions and assumptions, and opening the field of computer science in new ways and for new groups of people. Acknowledging our own privileged and subjective perspectives on computer science (we are insiders to the field), we do enjoy the nostalgia of the 1980s geek culture. Taking an honest and dedicated interest in computer science retro and nostalgia as a playful and creative way to scaffold new types of engaged interactions can assist equity initiatives in changing from within. By rewriting the history of computing to include the invisible women through intertextual design (Bjørn and Rosner 2021), the first author worked closely with Daniela Rosner in creating AtariWomen artefacts that manifest the important contributions of women in the early days of the computing gaming industry. We use these AtariWomen artefacts as a vehicle to bring in past stories about the women in gaming to the present with the aim of impacting the future of computer game development (ibid.).

There is a need for multiple parallel narratives about computer science – and computer scientists – that can coexist and benefit each other. Our agenda is not – and has never been – about making things 'womanly' or painting technology 'pink'. Instead, in each activity, in each design artefact, in each intervention, we always consider how our intervention designed with inclusivity in mind will be perceived by everyone. We want everyone to find the new learnings, abilities, technological artefacts, designs, and interventions made for and together with commonly underrepresented groups interesting, and thus to appreciate the inherent qualities of the technological artefacts.

> We propose that organizations actively work towards identifying and challenging stereotypes, not just as part of branding and communication but, more importantly, in the organization culture, considering all the stereotypical markers present in artefacts, technologies, and organizational layout, and that explicit interventions allowing for multiple parallel narratives can coexist.

Equity Mainstreaming

Gender mainstreaming has in recent years been a political approach adopted by the EU and the UN to measure and consider gender equity (Daly 2005). Inspired by this term, we propose *equity mainstreaming* to extend the focus from gender to the multiple diversity dimensions relevant to technology design. Equity mainstreaming in tech organizations and computer science departments is related to people, work processes, and the actual work of designing IT systems.

Equity mainstreaming includes diversity data collection. Collecting data about the state of diversity is not a simple task, and often organizations lack access to and insights into current situations, which also makes it difficult to evaluate whether new initiatives have the expected impact (Bjørn and Borsotti 2021). Often diversity data are limited to binary stats about women and men. In many situations, there are no data available across diversity dimensions, and the lack of data makes it difficult for decision-makers to consider intersectionality. As we argued in Chap. 7, classifications and categories have politics (Suchman 1994; Bowker and Star 2002; Bjørn and Balka 2007), which means that the categories and classifications we have for data collection and analysis considering diversity also have politics. By choosing to collect certain data while omitting other types of data – by making it possible to combine certain data and omit others – organizations make choices (maybe unintentionally) not only about what is visible and what remains invisible in the organization but also about what is excluded and what is included. For example, when job-posting software systems require applicants to state their gender as one of just two categories, applicants who identify as non-binary are forced to fit into this classification. Besides forcing applicants into categories they do not identify with, the system also renders invisible important insights about gender diversity in hiring. Further, if the classification of sexual harassment cases in an organization does not specify the situation and location of an event, it is difficult to act to prevent future harassment. Differently, if we knew from the data that harassment cases most often took place during social rather than professional events, and whether there are special locations and areas of the organization that are more prone to harassment situations, this would provide important insights for the organization to act on. Collecting detailed, yet anonymous, data about harassment might show how the introduction of technology blurring the barriers between work and private life produces new risks of workplace harassment (Tenorio and Bjørn 2019).

Available diversity statistics are essential for organizations to make strategies for inclusive environments. We need access to diversity statistics in order to make diversity data visibly available within the organization, emphasizing that diversity is important to its agenda. While diversity data are a multiplicity, not easily collected in a template, we have identified three main types of relevant diversity data, both quantitative and qualitative: *retention and career development* data to help organizations help everyone succeed within the organization; *harassment and discrimination* data to help organizations understand the contextual nature of events and to work towards reducing the risks; and *organizational citizenship* data to help organizations balance important service and care work required to function while reducing the risk of cultural taxation for under-represented groups (Bjørn and Borsotti 2021). Combining these data sources, while considering various diversity dimensions as well as intersectionality (Crenshaw 1989), will allow organizations to make interventions that support diversity and to consider how to use the data to inform them about important qualities of individuals that are often overlooked in promotion cases. Further, collecting data that can help the organization improve productivity for specific groups, such as neurodivergent software engineers, would also be beneficial.

Equity mainstreaming is about improving the work environment for all and utilizing opportunities for innovative thinking that accompany increased diversity. Technology design is fundamentally built on classification and categorization schemes and on processes by which users are often configured in resemblance to designers (I-methodology). These biased processes can affect the interface design and testing, database structures, and procedural design of, for example, workflow systems. Organizations should both increase diversity in software engineering teams and provide them the space, power, and resources to promote actual change – to identify and extend the edge cases and complex combinations of categories required for the IT systems being implemented. For example, in designing IT systems for interaction between schools and parents, software developers need to consider the wide variety of family constructions in a society such as "rainbow" families, single parents, or divorced parents (see Chap. 7). Having a diverse software engineering team increases the chances that different participants can provide different insights into the complex nuances of family structures, improving the quality of the system's data structure. Further, having a diverse team will also reduce the risk of overlooking important aspects of technology design such as how light reflects differently on different skin colors, constraining people with darker skin to interact with certain digital systems (Benjamin 2019a, b). Values and ethics are hugely important for the design of IT systems (Møller et al. 2020). In this way, introducing equity agendas to tech organizations and computer science education programs also means improving the curriculum in computing and the ethical aspects of technology design. Such initiatives will contribute to reducing the risk of discrimination by design (Sachs 2015; Rubin 2017).

Finally, equity mainstreaming in tech organizations can be used as a vehicle for tech innovation. Using diversity as a vehicle for tech innovation has particularly been emphasized in research on accessibility in technology design, where amazing researchers such as Katta Spiel, Kathrin Gerling, Cynthia Bennett, Emeline Brule, Rua Williams, Jennifer Rode, and Jennifer Mankoff (Spiel et al. 2020) have for years demonstrated how designing technology for people with a disability is an innovative way to develop technologies for all. For example, Cynthia Bennett demonstrates how the experiences of blindness and interaction with technology can be used to re-imagine technology design (Bennett et al. 2019). Over the years, accessibility research has argued for how tech experiments and user studies should include people with disabilities, since assessing, for example, a website using screen readers will allow software engineers to make their technologies more accessible and available – improving technology use for all.

> We propose to implement equity mainstreaming both as a strategy for improving the work environment in tech organizations and educational settings, increasing the diversity of employees and students, and as a strategy for technology design. Using equity mainstreaming in technology design requires considerations of categories and classification schemes, ethics, and how to account for diverse user groups when designing and implementing IT systems in society, improving technology use for all.

Chapter 9
Final Reflections

Working on research in equity, inclusion, and diversity in technology development has brought us many interesting reflections on the kinds of research we do, what we include, and what we exclude – and on the kind of institutions we are part of, were part of earlier, and will take an active part in creating in the future.

Misunderstanding FemTech

In re-reading reviews of early manuscripts for FemTech research, we see that we have often been misunderstood. Reviewers would expect and understand our work as developing new learning methods for STEM education, and we have often been asked to revise our research papers accordingly and advised to submit to conferences in education rather than computer science. For example, we might get statements such as: "*related work that is missing from other fields such as learning science, CSE, and STEM education*" in the reviews of our work (anonymized review). Demonstrating and arguing that our work is not about developing the field of learning science, computer science engineering, or STEM education – but instead about subverting norms and introducing institutional change in computer science as a community – has been a difficult task. Our work is directed at changing material and symbolic representations of computer science, as well as narratives about computing – and at opening the field through design activities, materials, and interactions based on the FemTech.dk design principles. Although it took us time to find ways to get our agenda understood, we have since received many invitations and much interest in our work both in Denmark and internationally, including invitations to present keynote talks at large conferences in Europe and North America as well as presentations at tech companies such as SAP, Microsoft, and Google. Further, some of these invitations have allowed us to publish in alternative and experimental venues such as Madeline Balaam and Lone Koefoed Hansen's

P. Bjørn et al., *Diversity in Computer Science*,
https://doi.org/10.1007/978-3-031-13314-5_9

collection *Wilful Technologies* (Balaam and Hansen 2019), where a version of GRACE is presented (Fig. 9.1).

These interactions with the international computer science community though invited talks and alternative publication venues have developed our knowledge, arguments, and design principles by allowing "outsiders" to engage with us around our alternative narratives developed inside the computer science department where they were created. This work of engaging with researchers and practitioners has also supported our agenda of changing the narrative, since by engaging with our work, we seek others to join our efforts. Our point here is that the impact of our work might not be visible via the 'ordinary' measures of academic production but instead has garnered much greater visibility outside 'ordinary' academic productions that might be more important when assessing the quality of research that includes advocacy and interventions. We conduct our research with the aim of long-term change – and if we evaluate the bare numbers of women students, they have increased; thus, from this perspective, we are succeeding. However, we would argue that our success cannot be reduced to the mere "numbers of women students", since the most important measure should be the change in institutions – the long-term change in the international computer science community. There is an increased focus on diversity, equity, and inclusion in computer science education and the profession worldwide, many people are doing work in this regard, and we are proud to add our small contribution to this endeavor.

Internal events and activities (such as workshops we organized for our faculty to reflect on how to use micro-controllers in teaching) were all important parts of the

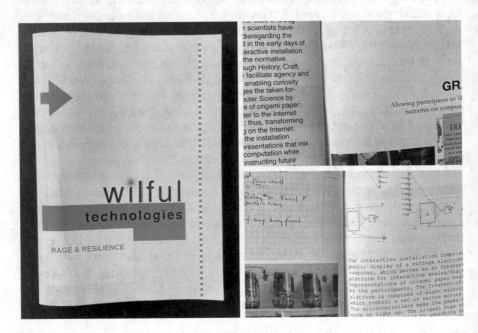

Fig. 9.1 Wilful technologies: race & resilience zine

transformation process of the institution; however, such activities require effort and resources to plan and execute, and when they do not directly add to ordinary measures of academic success, they easily end up as cultural taxation. The time and effort spent on departmental citizenship is crucial to transforming an organization towards equity and inclusion, but it also takes time away from research. Given that academic currency in terms of papers, grants, and citations is what makes or breaks an academic career, it also means that time not spent in these areas risks jeopardizing academic promotions and careers. Thus, throughout our FemTech research, we have also kept 'alternative' research streams alive, which then have served as the 'bread and butter' of our academic CVs. While we put in effort to align the different research streams we engaged with – for example, we researched makerspaces and open design (Menendez-Blanco and Bjørn 2019) – engaging in the important FemTech organizational work took time otherwise spent on academic merits.

Saying No to Window Dressing

Being aware of the risk of cultural taxation, we carefully discussed and reflected, each time we were asked to plan, join, or otherwise engage with people outside and inside the organization, whether a particular event would benefit the larger research agenda or just take time away for our already very occupied workdays. Saying 'no' is difficult in academia, but it is important to remember that each time you say no to something, you say yes to yourself, and the sparsest resource for a researcher is time. This meant that when someone asked us to join a podcast, a radio program, a talk, et cetera, we would consider whether the event was genuinely addressing the diversity and inclusion agenda through actions or was just 'window dressing' for events such as International Women's Day or Ada Lovelace Day. We did not want to use our sparse time if an event did not add to the existing agenda, and if organizations – such as companies or unions – did not take the agenda seriously. Finding ways to interrogate potential external invitations for events to determine whether we shared common ground is an important learning when doing equity work.

Mentoring and Bias Training Alone Will Not Foster Change

Transforming an organization towards equity and inclusion is many things and requires work by everyone. Liza Reisel, deputy project manager of the Nordic Centre of Excellence on Gender Equality in Research and Innovation, classifies the equity initiatives into four main categories: (1) network and mentor programs, (2) awareness-raising, (3) organizational change, and (4) affirmative action. Reisel and her colleagues found that while initiatives 1 and 2 often are the main ones implemented as strategies for transforming organizations, they do not foster long-term change in the Nordic countries. The problems here are not linked to a general prejudice against women, and networking and mentor programs are fine but not really doing the fundamental work required. Instead, Reisel cited by Højsgaard (2022) argues that having long-term effects on diversity requires effort and resources spent on organizational change anchored in high management at the institutions. In academia this would be at the vice-chancellor, dean, and department-head levels. Without attention and focus from decision-makers ensuring that equity, diversity, and inclusion are 'mainstreamed' into all parts and aspects of an organization, institutions and organizations will not be able to change. What does this really mean in practice?

Equity Is About Real Opportunity and Building CVs

In academia, as we have already mentioned, building a CV to ensure academic promotion requires papers, grants, and citations. However, as we also mentioned in the beginning of this book, the fundamental conditions for successful academic currency that serve this agenda of CV-building are based on researchers' privilege in supervising PhD students, which again is based on researchers' luck in winning external funding and grants. Academics can be viewed as entrepreneurial actors, situating themselves and navigating multiple interlinked opportunities and barriers, finding ways to win grants, allowing them to move towards their academic ambition. In this navigation work, opportunities such as awards, recognized prestige roles, and invitations play subtle yet crucial roles in building the academic CV. Winning a small grant or an award early in an academic career is a stepping stone to the next award and grant. What happened in an academic's past matters for the present state of the academic's CV and determines the potential of their future academic career. This means that management of academic institutions must take seriously their role as decision-makers with respect to diversity and equity when nominating, promoting, proposing, et cetera, researchers at all levels to ensure career development for the individual through building their CV.

In academic management, some of the leadership opportunities that need to be distributed in the organization support people's CVs, whereas others do not. For example, participating in an equity committee does not count in the same way that participating in a research committee does. Receiving an award for equity work is not as prestigious as receiving an award for research. Moreover, awards for equity work are often tokens, like a cup, whereas awards for research entail money.

Giving the estimated value of the work matters, and while we here provide examples from academia, there are similar incentives in industry and the public sector for what is viewed as valued, and how. Studying the organizational behaviors of mixed gender work organizations Linda Babcock, Maria Recalde, and Lise Vesterlund found that women disproportionally are expected to volunteer and accept to volunteer (Babcock et al. 2018) – for what has recently been labeled as "non-promotable tasks" (Babcock et al. 2022). Non-promotable tasks are tasks which are important for the organization but does not add to a person's CV. Equity work takes effort and time, and to do it right, management must carefully consider how to share leadership opportunities that count and how to acknowledge and value the leadership opportunities that do not really count but are important for the organization. Equity work *cannot* be a non-promotable task, if organizations truly want to change. Organizations must find ways to make essential equity work matter not just as extra work but as core to the organization and thus as adding value for promotion. Further, as part of the organization equity activities, it is essential that managers make sure to propose a diverse set of people for awards, allow them opportunities to sit on core prestige committees, and in general ensure that they can take advantage of leadership opportunities. If participating in a committee will benefit a person's CV, organizations must find ways to ensure that people who historically have not held leadership positions are proposed for such opportunities.

The Myth of Meritocracy

Besides considering how to share with equity new opportunities for career advancement between people in an organization, management also needs to consider current evaluation schemes or protocols for evaluating contributions. Special attention should be given to how to evaluate contributions that do not fit current evaluation schemes or protocols. Such initiatives need to take different forms depending on the organization and their work; however, to explain what we mean, we will use academia as an example.

In academia, evaluation schemes and protocols include measures often referred to as academic meritocracy. Academic meritocracy is based on the idea that if you do excellent research and work hard, you will succeed. Referring to the qualitative analysis of academic recruitment practices in the Netherlands by Van den Brink (2010), Mathias Nielsen (2016) explains how academic recruitment and selection processes are practices which 'mobilize masculinities' without academic decision-makers being fully aware of these practices:

> [The] theoretical concept 'mobilizing masculinities' [is] a starting point for exploring how male (and female) academics practice networking in recruitment and selection processes. The study illustrates a multiplicity of gender practices affecting who is invited to apply for research positions, whose reputations are built, and whose visibility is promoted through the recommendations of eminent (male) colleagues. While the authors note that such practices are clearly acknowledged by the recruiters as being intrinsic to the academic promotion game, their gendered consequences do not arise from conscious choices. (Nielsen 2016, p. 388)

Formal and inform network ties appear to be critical to academic recruitment and hiring but matter differently for women and men. Promotions, awards, and grants in academia often involve recommendations of academic referees; thus, the need for sponsorship is a crucial part of using the network (Bagilhole and Goode 2001). Bagilhole and Goode argue that success in academia is a socialization process involving reliance on colleagues for collaboration, friendship, and co-authorship.

Further, they show that success in academia requires self-promotion and that men scientists are often good at promoting not only themselves and also other men – but occasionally also other women (ibid.). Marianne Ferber studied academic citation practices and found that women tend to cite other women researchers more than men cite women, which, again, they argue, creates a larger citation gap between researchers of different genders (Ferber 1988). Both women and men cite the work of men, but only women cite the work of women. Ferber suggests that the problem of lack of recognition (lack of citations) is more severe when 'out-of-group' numbers are low – and that if these numbers increase, out-of-group participants will increasingly find it easier to gain acceptance (ibid.). Ferber's research indicates that citation numbers are not about research quality but are instead linked to the fact that the majority in most academic fields are men, and that they tend to quote other men. The closed successful sponsor network is thus not only about collaboration and co-authorship but also about mutual promotion practices as well as citation sharing.

From Gender to Intersectionality

We extend the analytical focus from a sole focus on gender to include other social identities and intersectionality. When women are cited less, non-White people are cited less, and people from the Global South are cited less, then women of color conducting research at a university in Africa are marginalized and rendered virtually invisible (Kumar and Karusala 2020). Affirmative actions within the international research communities such as citational justice, increasing the diversity in awards committees and paper selection committees, and decreasing costs and financial support for attending large conferences are required to make a change.

The streamlining of research – whereby a few highly cited researchers with a history of winning grants, supervising PhD students and post-docs, and being the last authors of an increasing number of publications that also cite prior publications, thus resulting in a steadily growing number of citations – risks only allowing for uniform and singular research following a certain template, reducing the plurality and multiplicity of the potential research questions that society needs to address. As expressed by Alon Zivony:

> Inequality inevitably leads to homogeneity of viewpoints and experiences, which limits our ability to ask new worthwhile questions and raises the risk of scientific stagnation. A fair evaluation system is therefore crucial not only from a social justice perspective, but also from a scientific standpoint. (Zivony 2019)

When we streamline our evaluation schemes and measuring protocols, we risk losing diverse perspectives and the ability to surprise each other with counter-narratives and productive debates. So what will it take to change this in academia?

We suggest that a place to begin this transformation is openness to the idea that the measuring of quality needs to consider how to evaluate and acknowledge different types of contributions to research, including how to consider merit. We should consider not analyzing people's CVs as objective measures but instead investigating the quality a person has achieved given the available resources. Graduating PhD students with many publications and citations from high-prestige institutions with high-prestige supervisors having many resources is less impressive than graduating PhD students who managed to do impressive work with few resources. However, even at high-prestige institutions that graduate PhD students from diverse backgrounds, these students will have had different conditions of success and failure based on their backgrounds and privileges.

Beyond Celebration of 'Women in Tech' Events

While we talk here about academia as the organizational unit, we suggest that similar structures, based on different metrics, are also at work in the tech industry. If we want to move beyond celebrating the need for "women in tech" at events in March each year, management in the tech industry and academia needs to take the problems seriously. It is management's responsibility to ensure the best possible conditions for all people having an interest in shaping the digital society of the future through engaging with computer science research and practice to succeed despite various intersectional diversity dimensions. This means that management must address and consider the distribution of promotional opportunities through the lens of equity, not equality. As long as people in computer science education or the tech industry, in the Nordic countries, lack equal conditions for access and success, it is management's responsibility to insist on the agenda in all organizational processes – and potentially consider how affirmative actions might be appropriate in specific situations to change the dynamics. Networking, mentoring, and learning about bias are not enough. We need equity mainstreaming in all areas of organizations, which requires critical analysis, creativity, cooperation, and management accountability.

Measurable Goals and Key Performance Indicators

This leads to the final reflection we would like to share based on our work: the reflection on numbers, goals, and measurement for success. If tech organizations and computer science education departments embark on a journey to transform their organizations to increased diversity, it is important that we develop measurable goals and markers that can help us navigate the challenging road and determine whether we are on the right path or need to take new initiatives.

The bare number of women versus men in an organization is not a good marker because it depends on the types of jobs these different groups of people fill. If we have an organization where all the women hold the administrative positions while the men hold the technical and leadership positions, we do not have a balanced workplace. Therefore, each organization must analyze and determine which measurable points allow management to pay attention and strategically shape a plan for diversity. In academia, one potential measure is increasing diverse faculty in the applicant pool for permanent faculty positions aiming at hiring 50% underrepresented groups in all new positions – and concrete activities could include specific faculty search protocols, new ways to post faculty positions, and protocols for inviting potential faculty to campus. Other potential measurements could be decreasing the gender gap for permanent high positions (full professors) considering a promotion path for existing underrepresented associate professors as well as including such initiatives as part of the hiring strategy. Ensuring that diverse faculty groups have access to PhD funding could be a concrete action, and here activities could include, besides fundraising from an institutional perspective, considerations of balanced co-financing and team PhD supervision. Such efforts could also include strategic use of awards and other CV-building activities, increasingly supporting diverse faculty in building their CVs.

Managerial monitoring of the ways that the distribution of academic citizenship and tasks are divided across faculty is important. Goals for this include defining a balance between responsibility for committee work critical for the institution and the people who do these tasks. In this work, knowledge of people's personal goals and strategies is important, to see whether there is any way the organization can support them. Last, more attention has to be directed to specific barriers experienced in academia by underrepresented groups, such as harassment and prejudice (Else 2021).

Diversity and equity efforts take work and resources. To succeed, organizations must develop organizational strategies where equity work is prioritized financially. We join others in stating that such efforts are crucial for computer science and the tech industry – since in the absence of diverse participation in the tech industry and academia, we risk jeopardizing democratic values and constrain certain populations in our digital technologies of tomorrow, intentionally or not. One could argue that, readers of this book occupying positions of power, now know about the risks, and inaction could be seen as an intentional neglect to act.

Equity, diversity, and inclusion are not a transformation process driven by the few members of marginalized groups. To succeed, we need collective action, which includes having people with decision power and responsibility lead the way.

References

Aagaard K, Kladakis A, Nielsen MW (2018) Concentration or dispersal of research funding. Quant Sci Stud 1(3):1–29

Abid A, Farooqi M, Zou J (2021) Persistent anti-muslim bias in large language models. Proceedings of the 2021 AAAI/ACM conference on AI, ethics, and society. Association for Computing Machinery, New York, p 298–306. https://doi.org/10.1145/3461702.3462624

Adam D (2019) Gamble on grants lotteries. Nature 575:574–575

Ahmed S (2012) On Being included: racism and diversity in institutional life. Duke University Press, Durham

Ahmed S (2016) Living a feminist life. Duke University Press, Durham

Akrich M (1995) User representations: practices, methods and sociology. In: Rip A, Misa T, Schot J (eds) Managing technology in society: the approach of constructive technology assessment. Pinter Publisher, London/New York, pp 167–184

Akrich M, Callon M, Latour B (2002a) The key to success in innovation Part 2: the art of choosing good spokespersons. Int J Innov Manag 6(2):207–225

Akrich M, Callon M, Latour B (2002b) The key to sucess in innovation Part 1: the art of interessement. Int J Innov Manag 6(2):187–206

Albusays K, Bjorn P, Dabbish L, Ford D, Murphy-Hill E, Serebrenik A, Storey M-A (2021) The diversity crisis in software development. IEEE Software 38(2):19–25

Alvarado D, Libeskind-Hadas R (2012) Broadening participation in computing at Harvey Mudd College. ACM Inroads 3(4):55–64

Alvarado C, Dodds Z, Libeskind-Hadas R (2012) Increasing women's participation in computing at Harvey Mudd College. ACM Inroads 3(4):55–64

Ames M, Bardzell J, Bardzell S, Lindtner S, Mellis D, Rosner D (2014) Making cultures: empowerment, participation, and demoncracy – or not? Panel: CHI: one of a CHInd. ACM, Toronto

Armstrong M, Jovanovic J (2015) Starting at the crossroads: intersectional approaches to institutionally supported underrepresented minorities women STEM faculty. J Women Minorities Sci Eng 21(2):141–157

Asbjørn Ammitzbøll Flügge T, Naja Holten Møller H (2021) Street-level algorithms and AI in bureaucratic decision-making: a caseworker perspective. Proceedings of the ACM on human-computer interaction (CSCW1), ACM.

Avison D, Lau F, Myers M, Nielsen PA (1999) Action research. Commun ACM 42(1):94–97

Babcock L, Recalde M, Vesterlund L (2018) Why women volunteer for task that don't lead to promotions. Harvard Business Review

Babcock L, Peyser B, Vesterlund L, Weingart L (2022) The no club: putting a stop to women's dead-end work. Piatkus, London

Baggersgaard C (2021) Topforskere: Træk lod om forskningsmidlerne. Forskerforum 340.

© The Author(s) 2023
P. Bjørn et al., *Diversity in Computer Science*,
https://doi.org/10.1007/978-3-031-13314-5

Bagilhole B, Goode J (2001) The contradiction of the myth of individual merit, and the reality of a patriarchal support system in academic careers: a feminist investigation. Eur J Women's Stud 8(2):161–180

Balaam M, Hansen LK (2019) Wilful technologies: a publishing experiment on feminist + technologies + design. Institut for Kommunikation og Kultur

Barad K (2003) Posthumanist performativity: toward an understanding of how matter comes to matter. Signs J Women Cult Soc 28(3):801–831

Bardzell, S. (2010) Feminist HCI: taking stock and outlining an agenda for design. CHI 2010 – The 28th annual CHI conference on human factors in computing systems. Atlanta

Bardzell S, Bardzell J (2011) Towards a feminist HCI methodology: social science, feminism, and HCI. Proceedings of the international conference on human factors in computing systems. Vancouver

Bardzell S, Rosner D, Bardzell J (2012) Crafting quality in design: integrity, creativity, and public sensibility. DIS'12: Proceedings of the designing interactive systems conference. Newcastle, p 11–20

Bardzell J, Bardzell S, Stolternan E (2014) Reading critical design: supporting reasoned interpretations of critical design. Proceedings of CHI'13. ACM Press, Toronto

Bardzell J, Bardzell S, Hansen LK (2015) Immodest proposals: research through design and knowledge. CHI 2015: Proceedings of the 33rd annual CHI conference on human factors in computing systems: crossings, Seoul, p 2093–2102

Bardzell J, Bardzell S, Dalsgaard P et al (2016) Documenting the research through design process. Proceedings of the 2016 ACM conference on designing interactive systems. Brisbane, p 96–107

Barry E (2021) Uber drivers say a 'racist' algorimhm is putting them out of work. Time *Magazine*. https://time.com/6104844/uber-facial-recognition-racist

Bell G, Blythe M, Sengers P (2005) Making by making strange: defamiliarization and the design of domestic technologies. ACM Trans Comput Hum Interact 12(2):149–173

Benjamin R (2016) Racial fictions, biological facts: expanding the sociological imagination through speculative methods. Catalyst Feminism Theory Technoscience 2

Benjamin R (2019a) Captivating technology: race, carceral technoscience, and liberatory imagination in everyday life. Duke University Press, Durham

Benjamin R (2019b) Race after technology: abolitionist tools for the new jim code. Polity Press, Cambridge

Bennett C, Peil B, Rosner D (2019) Biographical prototypes: reimagining recognition and disability in design. DIS'19: Proceedings of the 2019 on designing interactive systems conference. San Diego

Binder T, Redström J (2006) Exemplary design research. Paper presented at the DRS wonderground conference

Bishop L (1999) Visible and invisible work: the emerging post-industrial employment relation. Comput Support Coop Work 8:115–126

Bjögvinsson E, Ehn P, Hillgren P-A (2012) Design things and design thinking: contemporary participatory design challenges. Des Issues 28(3):101–116

Bjorgvinsson E, Ehn P, Hillgren P-A (2010) Participatory design and 'democratizing innovation'. Proceedings of the 11th biennial participatory design conference, ACM digital library. Sydney, p 41–50

Bjørn P (2012) Bounding practice: how people act in sociomaterial practices. Scand J Inf Syst 24(2):97–104

Bjørn, P. (2014) Sociomaterial-design in global software development: position paper presented at workshop on global software development in a CSCW perspective. Baltimore

Bjørn P (2019) Dark agile: global software development risk perceiving people as assets, not as humans. In: Sadowki C, Zimmermann T (eds) Rethinking Productivity in Software Engineering. Apress, New York

Bjørn P, Balka E (2007) Health care categories have politics too: unpacking the managerial agendas of electronic triage systems. ECSCW 2007: Proceedings of the Tenth European conference on computer supported cooperative work. Springer, Limerick

Bjørn P, Borsotti V (2021) Vores blotte tilstedeværelse som kvindelige IT-forskere er ikke nok til at skabe langvarig forandring. Altinget.dk January 22 & DIKU.dk.

Bjørn P, Boulus N (2011) Dissenting in reflective conversations: critical components of doing action research. Action Res J 9(3):282–302

Bjørn P, Boulus-Rødje N (2015) The multiple intersecting sites of design in CSCW research. Comput Support Coop Work 24(3):319–351

Bjørn P, Boulus-Rødje N (2018) Intrastructural inaccessibility: tech entrepreneurs in occupied Palestine. ACM Trans Comput Hum Interact 25(5):31

Bjørn P, Hornbæk K (2017) UCPH makerspace start-up meeting. Uniavisen.

Bjørn P, Markussen R (2013) Cyborg heart: the affective apparatus of bodily production of ICD patients. Sci Technol Stud 26(2)

Bjørn P, Menendez-Blanco M (2019) FemTech: broadening participation to digital technology development. Proceedings of the 27th ACM international conference on multimedia

Bjørn P, Østerlund C (2009) Materiality in hospital work: comparative study of the work in two pediatric emergency departments. AMCIS workshop paper. San Fransisco

Bjørn P, Østerlund C (2014) Sociomaterial-design: bounding technologies in practice. Springer, New York

Bjørn P, Rosner D (2021) Intertextual design: the hidden stories of atari women. Hum Comput Interact 37:370–395

Bjørn P, Burgoyne S, Crompton V, MacDonald T, Pickering B, Munro S (2009) Boundary factors and contextual contingencies: configuring electronic templates for health care professionals. Eur J Inf Syst 18:428–441

Bjørn P, Søderberg A-M, Krishna S (2017) Translocality in global software development: the dark side of global agile. Hum Comput Interact 34(2):174–203

Blomberg J, Karasti H (2013) Reflections on 25 years of ethnography in CSCW. Comput Support Coop Work 22(4-6):373–423

Blomberg J, Giacomi J, Mosher A, Swenton-Hall P (1993) Ethnographic field methods and their relation to design. In: Schuler D, Namioka A (eds) Participatory design: principles and practices. Lawrence Erlbaum Associates Publisher, London, UK, pp 123–155

Blythe M, Andersen K, Clarke R, Wright P (2016) Anti-solutionist strategies: seriously silly design fiction. CHI'16: Proceedings of the 2016 CHI conference on human factors in computing systems. Association for Computing Machinery. New York, p 4968–4978

Bødker S (2015) Third-wave HCI, 10 years later – participation and sharing. Interaction 22(5):24–31

Bødker S, Ehn P, Knudsen J, Kyng M, Madsen KH (1988) Computer support for cooperative design. Conference on computer-supported cooperative work (CSCW). Portland

Bødker S, Ehn P, Sjögren D, Sundblad Y (2000) Co-operative design – perspectives on 20 years with 'the Scandinavian IT design model'. Kungl Tekniska Hogskolan, Stockholm

Bødker K, Kensing F, Simonsen J (2004) Participatory IT design: designing for business and workplace realities. The MIT Press, Cambridge

Borsotti V, Bjørn P (2022) Humor and stereotypes in computing: an equity-focused approach to institutional accountability. Conference on computer supported cooperative work, vol 31

Boulus-Rødje N (2012) Action research as a network: collective production of roles and interventions. 20th European conference on information systems (ECIS). Barcelona

Boulus-Rødje N (2018) In search for the perfect pathway: supporting knowledge work of welfare workers. Comput Support Coop Work 27:841–874

Boulus-Rødje N, Bjørn P (2015) Design challenges in supporting distributed knowledge: an examination of organizing elections. CHI'15: Proceedings of the 33rd annual ACM conference on human factors in computing systems. Seoul

Boulus-Rødje N, Bjørn P (2019) Digital (Occupied) Palestine. With an eye to the future: HCI research and practice in the arab world.

Boulus-Rødje N, Bjørn P (2021) Tech public of Erosion: the formation and transformation of the Palestinian tech entrepreneurial public. Comput Supported Coop Work 31:299–339

Boulus-Rødje N, Bjørn P, Ghazawneh A (2015) "It's about business, not politics": an ethnographic study of an Israeli-Palestinian web start-up. International conference of critical geography. Rammallah

Bowker GC, Star SL (2002) Sorting things out: classification and its consequences. The MIT Press, Cambridge

Boyd D (2007) Why youth heart social network sites: the role of networked publics in teenage social life. The Berkman Center for internet & society research publication series: the social science research network electronic paper collection research publication no. 2007-16

Brennan A, Chugh JS, Kline T (2002) Traditional versus open office design: a longitudinal field study. Environ Behav 34(3):279–299

Breslin S, Wadhwa B (2014) Exploring nuanced gender perspectives within the HCI community. Proceedings of the India HCI 2014 conference on human computer interaction. New Delhi

Buechley L, Hill M (2010) LilyPad in the wild: how hardware's long tail is supporting new engineering an design communities. ACM conference on designing interactive systems, p 199–207

Buechley L, Eisenberg M, Catchen J., Crockett A (2008) The LilyPad Arduino: using computational textiles to investigate engagement, aesthetics, and divers. Proceedings of the SIGCHI conference on human factors in computing systems. ACM, Florence, p 423–432

Bundsgaard J, Bindslev S, Caeli EN, Pettersson M, Rusmann A (2018) Danske elevers teknologoforståelse: Resultater fra ICILS-undersøgelsen. Århus Universitetsforlag

Buolamwini J, Gebru T (2018) Gender shades: intersectional accuracy disparities in commercial gender classification. Proceedings of the 1st conference on fairness, accountability and transparency, in PMLR, vol 81, p 77–91

Butler J (1999) Gender trouble: feminism and the subversion og identity. Routledge, New York/London

Buxton B (2010) Sketching user experiences: getting the design right and the right design. Morgan Kaufmann

Çakır NA, Gass A, Foster A, Lee FJ (2017) Development of a game-design workshop to promote young girls' interest towards computing through identity exploration. Comput Educ 108:115–130

Cheryan S, Plaut V, Davies P, Steele C (2009) Ambient belonging: how stereotypical cues impact gender participation in computer science. J Pers Soc Psychol 97(6):1045

Cheryan S, Plaut V, Handron C, Hudson L (2013) The steriotypical computer scientist: gendered media representations as a barrier to inclusion for women. Sex Roles 69(1–2):58–71

Christophersen M, Mørck P, Langhoff TO, Bjørn P (2015) Unforeseen challenges: adopting wearable health data tracking devices to reduce health insurance costs in organizations. Human-computer interaction international conference (HCII). Springer. Los Angeles

Chrousos G, Mentis A-F (2020) Imposter syndrome threatens diversity. Science 367(6479):749–750

Clance PR, Imes S (1978) The imposter phenomenon in high achieving women: dynamics and therapeutic interventions. Psychother Theory Res Pract 15(3)

Crenshaw K (1988) Race, reform, and retrenchment: transformation and legitimation in antidiscrimination law. Harv Law Rev 101(7):1331–1387

Crenshaw K (1989) Demarginalizing the intersection of race and sex: a black feminist critique of antidescrimination doctrine, feminist theory and antiracist politics. Univ Chic Leg Forum 1989(1):8

Dalsgaard P (2016) Experimental Systems in research through design. Proceedings of the 2016 CHI conference on human factors in computing systems. San Jose

Daly M (2005) Gender mainstreaming in theory and practice. Soc Polit Int Stud Gend State Soc 12(3):433–450

Dann WP, Cooper S, Pausch R (2006) Learning to program with Alice. Prentice Hall Press, Hoboken

Dantec CL, DiSalvo C (2013) Infrastructuring and the formation of publics in participatory design. Soc Stud Sci 43(2):241–264

Dastin J (2018) Amazon scraps secret AI recruiting tool that showed bias against women. Reuters

DataHub (2019) Equal measures 2030: harnessing the power of data for gender equality: introducing the 2019 EM2030 SDG gender index. EM2030 Data Hub: www.data.em2030.org/2019-global-report

D'Ignazio C, Klein LF (2020) Data feminism. MIT Press, Cambridge

DIKU (2021) Historien om Danmarks første datalogiske institut. https://di.ku.dk/ominstituttet/dikus-historie/

DIKU (2022) DIKU's FemTech workshops

Disalvo C (2012) Adversarial design. MIT Press, Cambridge/London

Disalvo C, Lodato T, Jenkins T, Lukens J, Kim T (2014) Making public things: How HCI design can express matters of concern. CHI'14: Proceedings of the SIGCHI conference on human factors in computing systems, Toronto

Disalvo C, Jenkins T, Lodato T (2016) Designing speculative civics. Proceedings of the 2016 CHI conference on human factors in computing systems, San Jose

Dourish P (2017) The stuff of bits: an essay on the materiality of information. MIT Press, Cambridge

Duplantis W, MacGregor E, Klawe M, Ng M (2002) Virtual family: an approach to introducing java programming. ACM SIGCSE Bull 34(2):40–43

Edelman B, Luca M, Svirsky D (2017) Racial discrimination in the sharing economy: evidence from a field experiment. Am Econ J Appl Econ 9(2):1–22

Else H (2021) Largest-ever survey exposes career obstacles for LGBTQ scientists. Nature. https://www.nature.com/articles/d41586-41021-00221-w

Ensmenger N (2010) The computer boys take over: computers, Programmers, and the politics of technical expertise. MIT Press, London

Enyedy N, Mukhopadhyay S (2007) They don't show nothing I didn't know: emergent tensions between culturally relevant pedagogy and mathematics pedagogy. J Learn Sci 16(2):139–174

Faulkner W (2000) Dualisms, hierachies and gender in engineering. Soc Stud Sci 30(5):759–792

Ferber M (1988) Citations and networking. Gend Soc 2(1):82–89

Fiebrink RA, TR Alcott (2003) Designing a programming workshop for girls. Retrieved January 17 2006. https://web.cse.ohio-state.edu/~bair.41/WIC/Designing_A_Programming_Workshop_For_Girls.pdf

Forskningsministeriet U-O (2021) Admitted students from 1997 through 2021

Forsythe D (1993) Using ethnography to build a working system: rethinking basic design assumptions. Proc Annu Symp Comput Appl Med Care 1993:505–509

Forsythe D (1999) It's just a matter of common sense: ethnography as invisible work. Comput Supported Coop Work 8(1–2):127–145

Forsythe D (2001) Studying those who study us: an anthropologist in the world of arteficial intelligence. Standford University Press, Standford

Forum WE (2020) Global gender gab report 2020. https://www3.weforum.org/docs/WEF_GGGR_2020.pdf

Fox S, Ulgado R, Rosner D (2015) Hacking culture, not devices: access and recognition in feminist hackerspaces. CSCW, Vancouver

Frandsen S (2022) The Novo Nordisk foundation will draw lots among applicants. Science Report. https://sciencereport.dk/penge/novo-nordisk-fonden-klar-med-stort-forsoeg

Frieze C, Quesenberry J (2013) From different to diversity: including women in the changing face of computing. SIGCSE'13: Proceeding of the 44th ACM technical symposium on Computer science education, Denver

Frieze C, Quesenberry J (2015) Kicking butt in computer science: women in computing at Carnegie Mellon University, Dog Ear Publishing

Frieze C, Quesenberry J (2019) Cracking the digital ceiling: women in computing around the world. Cambridge University Press, Cambridge

Fuchsberger V, Murer M, Tscheligi M, Lindtner S, Reiter A, Bardzell S, Bardzell J, Bjørn P (2015) The future of making: where industrial and personal fabrication meet. Workshop paper at critical alternatives. Århus. https://projects.hci.sbg.ac.at/fabrication2015/organizers/

Fuchsberger V, Murer M, Tscheligi M, Lindtner S, Bardzell S, Bardzell J, Reiter A, Bjorn P (2016) Fabrication & HCI: hobbyist making, industrial production, and beyond. Proceedings of the 2016 CHI conference extended abstracts on human factors in computing systems. ACM, San Jose, p 3550–3557

Gaver W (2012) What should we expect from research through design. HI'12 Proceedings of the SIGCHI conference on human factors in computing systems, p 937–946

Glaser BG, Strauss AL (1967) The discovery of grounded theory: strategies for qualitative research. Aldine De Gruyter, New York

Goodman E, Stolterman E, Wakkary R (2011) Understanding interaction design practices. Proceedings of the SIGCHI conference on human factors in computing systems, p 1061–1070

Hall O (2020) Forsikringsselskaber har i årevis diskrimineret gravide ulovligt. Men nu skal det være slut. Danish Broadcast station. DR.DK

Hallnäs L, Redström J (2001) Slow technology–designing for reflection. Pers Ubiquit Comput 5(3):201–212

Hamidi F, Scheuerman MK, Branham S (2018) Gender recognition or gender reductionism? The social implications of automatic gender recognition systems. CHI'18: Proceedings of the 2018 CHI conference on human factors in computing systems, Montreal

Hansen E (1997) En koral i tidens strøm, Roskilde Universitetsforlag

Haraway D (1987) Donna Haraway reads "the national geographic" on primates. Youtube video http://www.youtube.com/watch?v=eLN2ToEIlwM

Haraway D (1990) A manifesto for cyborgs: science, technology, and socialist feminism in the 1980s. In: Nicholson L (ed) Feminism/Postmodernisme. Routlegde, New York/London

Haraway D (1991) Simians, cyborgs and women: the reinvention of nature. Free Associations Books, London

Haraway D (1994) A game of cat's cradle: science studies, feminist theory, cultural studies. Configurations 2(1):59–71

Hariri YA, Magdy W, Wolters MK (2021) Atheists versus theists: religious polarisation in arab online communities. Proceedings of the ACM on human-computer interaction, vol 5, p 1–28

Henwood F (2000) From the woman question in technology to the technology question in feminism: rethinking gender equality in IT education. Eur J Women's Stud 7(2):209–227

Hertz G (2012) Critical making. Telharmnonium Press

Hicks M (2017) Programmed Inequality: how Britain descarded women technologists and lost its edge in computing. MIT Press

Højsgaard L (2022) Ligestillingstiltag mod bias gør ingen forskel. Forskerforum 2(March 2022):4–5

Holman L, Stuard-Fox D, Hauser C (2018) The gender gab in science: how long until women are equally represented? PLoS Biol 16. https://doi.org/10.1371/journal.pbio.2004956

Hornung D, Müller C, Shklovski I, Jakobi T, Wulf V (2017) Navigating relationships and boundaries: concerns around ICT-uptake for elderly people. Proceedings of the 2017 CHI conference on human factors in computing systems, p 7057–7069

Huffman AH, Whetten J, Huffman WH (2013) Using technology in higher education: the influence of gender roles on technology self-efficacy. Comput Hum Behav 29(4):1779–1786

Jenkins T, Dantec CAL, DiSalvo C, Lodato T, Asad M (2016) Object-oriented publics. Proceedings of the SIGCHI conference on human factors in computing systems, p 827–839

Jensen RE, Bjørn P (2012) Divergence and convergence in global software development: cultural complextities as societal structures. COOP: design of cooperative systems. Springer, p 123–136

Joseph T, Hirshfield L (2011) Why don't you get somebody new to do it? Race and cultural taxation in the academy. Ethn Racial Stud 34(1):121–141

Karasti H (2001) Bridging work practice and system design: integrating systemic analysis, appreciative intervention and practitioners participation. Comput Supported Coop Work 10:211–246

Kelleher C, Pausch R (2006) Lessons learned from designing a programming system to support middle school girls creating animated stories. Report 165–172

Kelleher C, Pausch R, Kiesler S (2007) Storytelling alice motivates middle school girls to learn computer programming. Proceedings of the SIGCHI conference on human factors in computing systems. Association for Computing Machinery, San Jose, p 1455–1464

Kensing F, Blomberg J (1998) Participatory design: issues and concerns. Comput Supported Coop Work 7(3-4):167–185

Keyes O (2018) The misgendering machines: Tran/HCI implications of automatic gender recognition. CSCW

Kircher MM (2017) Gender discrimination at Uber is a reminder of how hard women have to fight to be believed. NyMag – select all http://nymag.com/selectall/2017/02/susan-fowler-alleges-sexual-discrimination-against-uber.html

Ko AJ, Oleson A, Ryan N, Register Y, Xie B, Tari M, Davidson M, Druga S, Loksa D (2020) It is time for more critical CS education. Commun. ACM 63, p 31–33

Koskinen I, Binder T, Redström J (2008) Lab, field, gallery, and beyond. Artif J Des Pract 2(1):46–57

Koskinen I, Zimmerman J, Binder T, Redstrom J, Wensveen S (2011) Design research through practice: from the lab, field, and showroom. Elsevier

Kristiansen KH, Valeur-Meller M, Dombrowski L, Møller NH (2018) Accountability in he blue collar data driven workplace. Proceedings of the 2018 CHI conference on human factors in computing systems, Montreal

Kruger A (1983) Welcome to the club. News paper article

Kumar N, Karusala N (2020) Braving citational justice within human-computer interaction. https://nehakumar.medium.com/braving-citational-justice-within-hci-5b43c1436fbc

Langford J, Clance P (1993) The imposter phenomenon: recent research findings regarding dynamics, personality and family patterns and their implications for treatment. Pschotherapy 30(3):495–501

Latour B (1987) Science in action: how to follow scientists and engineers through society. Harvard University, Cambridge

Law J, Singelton V (2014) ANT, multiplicity and policy. Crit Policy Stud 8(4):370–396

Lewin K (1946) Action research and minority problems. J Soc Issues 2(4):34–46

Löwgren J, Larsen HS, Hobye M (2013) Jonas Löwgren, HeNrIK SvArrer LArSeN, and Mads Hobye. 2013. Towards programmatic design research. Des Learn 6:1–2

Lundberg EH, von der Osten JP, Kanto R, Bjørn P (2017) The hackerspace manifested as a DIY-IoT entity: shaping and protecting the identity of the community. Proceedings of 15th European conference on computer-supported cooperative work – exploratory papers. The European Society for Socially Embedded Technologies. Sheffield (ISSN 2510-2591)

Madsen EB, Aagaard K (2020) Concentration of Danish research funding on individual researchers and research topics: patterns and potential drivers. Quant Sci Stud 1(3):1159–1181

Maloney J, Resnick M, Rusk N, Silverman B, Eastmond E (2010) The Scratch programming language and environment. ACM Trans Comput Hum Edu 10(16):15

Mankoff J, Hayes G, Kasnitz D (2010) Disability studies as a source of critical inquiri for the field of assistive technology. ASSETS. ACM, Orlando

Margolis J, Fisher A (2003) Unlocking the clubhouse: women in computing. MIT Press

Mark G, Lyytinen K, Bergman M (2007) Boundary objects in design: an ecological view of design artifacts. J Assoc Inf Syst 8(11):34

Markus ML (1983) Power, politics, and MIS implementation. Commun ACM 26(6):430–444

Marres N (2007) The issues deserve more credit pragmatist contributions to the study of public involvement in controversy. Soc Stud Sci 37(5):759–780

Martin D, Hanrahan B, O'Neill J, Gupta N (2014) Being a turker. CSCW2014. ACM, Baltimore

Mathiassen L (1998) Reflective system development. Scand J Inf Syst 10(1&2):67–134

Mathiassen L (2002) Collaborative practice research. Inf Technol People 15(4):321–345

Matthiesen S, Bjørn P (2016) Let's look outside the office: analytical lens unpacking collaborative relationships in global work. COOP 2016. Springer, Trento

Matthiesen S, Bjørn P (2017) When distribution of tasks and skills are fundamentally problematic: a failure story from global software outsourcing. PACM on human-computer interaction: online first 2018 ACM conferencc on computer-supported cooperative woek and social computing, vol 1(2, Article 74), p 16

Matthiesen S, Bjørn P, Trillingsgaard C (2020) Attending to implicit bias as a way to move beyond negative steriotyping in GSE. ICGSE'20: Proceedings of the 15th international conference on global software engineering

Matthiesen S, Bjørn P, Trillingsgaard C (2022) Implicit bias and negative stereotyping in global software development and why it is time to move on! J Soft Evol Process:e2435

Mayer AL, Tikka PM (2008) Family-friendly policies and gender bias in academia. J High Educ Policy Manag 30(4):363–374

Mellström U (2009) The intersection of gender, race and cultural boundaries, or why is computer science in Malaysia dominated by women? Soc Stud Sci 39(6):885–907

Menéndez M, Bjørn P, Angeli AD (2017) Critical design artefacts: enacting alternative political agendas. ACM CSCW computer supported cooperative work, Portland

Menendez-Blanco M, Angeli AD (2016) Matters of concern as design opportunities. In: De Angeli A, Bannon L, Marti P, Bordin S (eds) COOP 2016: Proceedings of the 12th international conference on the design of cooperative systems. Springer, Trento

Menendez-Blanco M, Bjørn P (2019) Makerspaces on social media: shaping access to open design. Hum Comput Interact 34:470–505

Menendez-Blanco M, Bjørn P, Møller NH, Bruun J, Dybkjær H, Lorentzen K (2018) GRACE: broadening narratives of computing through history, craft and technology Demo paper, ACM GROUP conference

Merton R (1968) The Matthew effect in science. Science 159(3810):56–63

Møller NH (2018) The future of clerical work is precarious. Interactions 25(4)

Møller NH, Vikkelsø S (2012) The clinical work of secretaries: exploaring the interaction of administrative and clinical work in the diagnosing process. COOP: from research to practice in the design of cooperative systems: results and open challenges. Springer, Grenoble, p 33–47

Møller NH, Bjørn P, Villumsen JC, Hancock T, Aritake T, Tani S (2017) Data tracking in search of workflows. ACM CSCW, Portland

Møller NH, Fitzpatrick G, Dantec CL (2019) Assembling the case: citizens' strategies for exercising authority and personal autonomy in social welfare. Proceedings of the ACM on human-computer interaction, vol 3 (GROUP)

Møller NH, Shklovski I, Hildebrandt T (2020) Shifting concepts of value: designing algorithmic decision-support systems for public services. Nordichi, Tallinn

Møller NH, Neff G, Simonsen JG, Villumsen JC, Bjørn P (2021a) Can workplace tracking ever empower? Collective sensemaking for the responsible use of sensor data at work. Proceedings of the ACM on human-computer interaction, vol 5 (GROUP)

Møller NHH, Nielsen TRR, Dantec CL (2021b) Work of the unemployed: an inquiry into individuals' experience of data usage in public services and possibilities for their agency. Designing interactive systems conference 2021, ACM

Morris MR, Begel A, Wiedermann B (2015) Understanding the challenges faced by neurodiverse software engineering employees: towards a more inclusive and productive technical workforce. ASSETS ACM, Lisbon

Muller M (2011) Feminism asks the 'who' questions in HCO. Interact Comput 23:447–449

Mumford E (2001) Advice for an action researcher. Inf Technol People 14(1):12–27

Mumford E (2006) The story of socio-technical design: reflections on its successes, failures and potential. Inf Syst J 16:317–342

Mustafa M, Lazem S, Alabdulqader E, Toyama K, Sultana S, Ibtasam S, Anderson R, Ahmed SI (2020) IslamicHCI: designing with and within Muslim populations. In extended abstracts of the 2020 CHI conference on human factors in computing systems (CHI EA'20). Association for Computing Machinery, New York, p 1–8. https://doi.org/10.1145/3334480.3375151

Nielsen M (2016) Limits to meritocracy? Gender in academic recruitment and promotion processes. Sci Public Policy 43(3):386–399

Nielsen TR, Møller NH (2020) Work of the 'unemployed': a design fiction. Proceedings of 18th European conference on computer-supported cooperative work

Noble SU (2018) Algorithms of oppression: how search engines reinforce racism. New York University Press

Norn MT (2019) Koncentration af konkurrenceudsatte forskningsmidler. DEA

Ogbonnaya-Ogburu IF, Smith ADR, To A, Toyama K (2020) Critical race theory for HCI. Proceedings of the 2020 CHI conference on human factors in computing systems. ACM, Honolulu

Orlikowski W (1992) Learning from notes: organizational issues in groupware implementation. Conference on computer supported cooperative work. ACM, New York

Orlikowski W (1995) Categories: concept, content and context. Comput Supported Coop Work 3:73–78

Orlikowski W (2007) Sociomaterial practices: exploring technology at work. Organ Stud 28(9):1435–1448

Orlikowski W, Scott S (2008) Sociomateriality: challenging the separation of technology, work, and organization. Acad. Manag Ann 2(1):433–474

Østerlund C, Bjørn P (2011) Socio-material infrastructure in emergency departmental work. Third international workshop on infrastructures in healthcare: global health. IT University of Copenhagen, Copenhagen

Oudshoorn N (2008) Diagnosis at a distance: the invisible work of patients and healthcare professionals in cardiac telemonitoring technology. Sociol Health Illn 30(2):272–288

Oudshoorn N, Rommes E, Stienstra M (2004) Configuring the user as everybody: gender and design cultures in information and communication technologies. Sci Technol Hum Values 29(1):30–63

Padilla A (1994) Ethnic minority scholars, research, and mentoring: current and future issues. Educ Res 23(4):24–27

Peek N, Coleman J, Moyer I, Gershenfeld N (2017) Cardboard Machine Kit: modules for the rapid prototyping of rapid prototyping machines. Proceedings of the 2017 CHI conference on human factors in computing systems. ACM, Denver

Petersen A, Cohn ML, Hildebrandt TT, Møller NH (2021) 'Thinking problematically' as a resource for ai design in politicised contexts. In CHItaly 2021: 14th biannual conference of the Italian SIGCHI Chapter

Pierce J, Senger P, Hirsch T, Jenkins T, Gaver W, Disalvo C (2015) Expanding and refining design and criticality in HCI. CHI'2015: Proceedings of the 33rd annual ACM conference on human factors in computing systems. ACM, Seoul, p 2083–2092

Pinkard N, Erete S, Martin CK, Royston MMD (2017) Digital youth divas: exploring narrative-driven curriculum to spark middle school girls' interest in computational activities. J Learn Sci 26(3):477–516

Possing B (2018) Argumenter imod kvinder. Strandberg Publishing

Potluri V, Vaithilingam P, Iyengar S, Vidhya Y, Swaminathan M, Srinivasa G (2018) CodeTalk: improving programming environment accessibility for visually impaired developers. CHI'18: Proceedings of the 2018 CHI conference on human factors in computing systems. ACM, Montréal

Preston AM (2021) Taking on tech: Dr. Timnit Gebru Exposes the underbelly of performative diversity in the tech industry. Forbes https://www.forbes.com/sites/forbestheculture/2021/07/30/taking-on-tech-dr-timnit-gebru-exposes-the-underbelly-of-performative-diversity-in-the-tech-industry/?sh=20c6659ff910.

Rankin Y, Thomas J (2019) Straighten up and fly right: rethinking intersectionality in HCI research. Interactions 26(6):64–68

Rankin Y, Thomas J (2020) The intersectional experiences of black women in computing. SIGCSE. ACM, Portland

Rapoport RN (1970) Three dilemmas in action research. Hum Relat 23(6):499–513

Raptis D, Jensen RH, Kjeldskov J, Skov M (2017) Aesthetic, functional and conceptual provocation in research through design. Proceedings of the 2017 conference on designing interactive systems, Edinburgh

Ratto M (2012) Critical making: conceptual and material studies in technology and social life. Inf Soc 12(31):37–41

Resnick M, Maloney J, Monroy-Hermandez A, Rusk N, Eastmond E, Brennan K, Millner A, Rosenbaum E, Silver J, Silverman B, Kafai Y (2009) Scratch: programming for all. Commun ACM 52(11):60–67

Richard G, Giri S (2017) Inclusive collaborative learning with multi-interface design: implications for diverse and equitable makerspace education. CSCL Proceedings, ISLS, p 415–455

Richard GT, Kafai YB, Adleberg B, Telhan O (2015) StitchFest: diversifying a college Hackathon to broaden participation and perceptions in computing. Proceedings of the 46th ACM technical symposium on computer science education, p 114–119

Rode J (2011) A theoretical agenda for feminist HCI. Interact Comput 23:393–400

Rodriguez SL, Lehman K (2017) Developing the next generation of diverse computer scientists: the need for enhanced, intersectional computing identity theory. Comput Sci Edu 27(3-4):229–247

Rosner D, Lindtner S, Erickson I, Forlano L, Jackson S, Kolko B (2014) Making cultures: building things & building communities. CSCW-companion. ACM, Baltimore

Rosner D, Friedman K, Stolterman E (2018a) Critical fabulations. The MIT Press, Cambridge

Rosner D, Shorey S, Craft B, Remick H (2018b) Making core memory: design inquiry into gendered legacies of engineering and craftwork. Proceedings of the 2018 CHI conference on human factors in computing systems

Rubin J (2017) Why does PayPal discriminate against Palestinian? The Electronic Intifada. https://electronicintifada.net/content/why-does-paypal-discriminate-against-palestinians/20611

Rubin J, Blackwell L, Conley T (2020) Fragile masculinity: men, gender, and online harassment. Proceedings of the 2020 CHI conference on human factors in computing systems

Sachs B (2015) UBER: a platform for discrimination? on labour: workers, unions, and politics. https://onlabor.org/2015/10/22/uber-a-platform-for-discrimination/

Sandberg S (2013) Lean. In: Women, work, and the will to lead. Knopf

Sax L, Blaney JM, Lehman KJ, Rodriguez SL, George K, Zavala C (2018) Sense of belonging in computing: the role of introductory courses for women and underrepresented minority students. Soc Sci 7(122)

Schaller R (1997) Moore's law: past, present and future. IEEE Spectr 34(6):52–59

Schlesinger A, Edwards WK, Grinter RE (2017) Intersectional HCI: engaging identity through gender, race, and class. CHI'17: Proceedings of the 2017 CHI conference on human factors in computing systems. Association for Computing Machinery, New York, p 5412–5427

Scott KA, Clark K, Hayes E, Mruczek C, Sheridan K (2010) Culturally relevant computing programs: two examples to inform teacher professional development. Society for information technology & teacher education international conference, p 1269–1277

Senger P, Boehner K, David S, Kaye JJ (2005) Reflective design. Aarhus'05, Denmark

Sharp H (2003) Interaction design. Wiley

Shorey S, Rosner D (2019) A voice of process: re-presencing the gendered labor of Apollo innovation. Communication + 17:4

Sicart M, Shklovski I (2020) Pataphysical software: (ridiculous) technological solutions for imaginary problems. DIS, Eindhoven

Spiel K, Gerling K, Bennett C, Brule E, Williams R, Rode J, Mankoff J (2020) Nothing about us without us: investigating the role of critical disability studies in HCI. CHIEA'20: extended abstracts of the 2020 CHI conference on human factors in computing systems

Sproull L, Kiesler S, Zubrow D (1984) Encountering an Alien culture. J Soc Issues 40(3):31–48

Star SL, Griesemer J (1989) Institutional ecology, translations and boundary objects: amateurs and professionals in Berkeleys museum of Vertebrate Zoology, 1907–1939. Soc Stud Sci 19:387–420

Star SL, Strauss A (1999) Layers of silence, arenas of voice: the ecology of visible and invisible work. Comput Supported Coop Work 8:9–30

Stickel O, Hornung D, Aal K, Rohde M, Wulf V (2015) 3D printing with marginalized children – an exploration in a Palestinian refugee camp. European conference on computer supported cooperative work (ECSCW). Springer, Oslo

Strohmeier P, Knibbe J, Boring S, Hornbæk K (2017) zPatch: hybrid resistive/capacitive eTextile input. Tangible, embedded, and embodied interaction (TEI). ACM, Stockholm

Suchman L (1994) Do categories have politics? The language/action perspective reconsidered. Comput Supported Coop Work 2(3):177–190

Suchman L (2003) Located accountabilities in technology production. Centre for Science Studies, Lancaster University

Suchman L (2007) Human-machine reconfigurations: plans and situated actions. Cambridge University Press, Cambridge

Sveinsdottir E, Frøkjær E (1988) Datalogy – the Copenhagen tradition of computer science. BIT 28:450–472

Tabel OL, Jensen J, Dybdal M, Bjørn P (2017) Programming as a social and tangible activity. Interactions November–December:70–73

Tanenbaum TJ, Williams A, Desjardins A, Tanenbaum K (2013) Democratiing technology: pleasure, utility and expressiveness in DIY and maker practice. CHI. ACM, Paris, p 2603–2612

Tellioğlu H, Lewkowicz M, Carvalho AFPD, Breškovic I, Schinkinger S, Tixier B (2014) Collaboration and Coordination in the Context of Informal Care (CCCiC) concepts, methods, and technologies. Proceedings of the 18th international conference on supporting group work, p 324–327

Tenorio N, Bjørn P (2019) Online harassment in the workplace: the role of technology in labour law disputes. Comput Supported Coop Work 28(3–4):293–315

Than EPPP, Herbsleb J, Nolte A, Gerber E, Fiore-Gartland B, Chapman B, Moser A, Wilkins-Diehr N (2018) The 2nd workshop on hacking and making at time-bounded events: current trends and next steps in research and event design. W35

Thorhauge C (2006) Regnecentralen – festen der aldrig sluttede. Prosabladet

Thyssen M (2015) Tackling youth unemployment: a top priority. European Commission, Speech. http://europa.eu/rapid/press-release_SPEECH-15-4716_en.htm

Tissenbaum M, Sheldon J, Abelson H (2019) From computational thinking to computational action. Commun ACM 62(3):34–36

Trauth EM (2002) Odd girl out: an individual differences perspective on women in the IT profession. Inf Technol People 15(2):98–118

Tulshyan R, Burey JA (2021) Stop telling women they have imposter syndrome. Harvard Business Review https://hbr.org/2021/02/stop-telling-women-they-have-imposter-syndrome

Valla JM, Williams W (2012) Increasing achievement and higher-education representation of under-represented groups in science, technology, engineering, and mathematics fields: a review of current K-12 intervention programs. J Women Minorities Sci Eng 18(1). https://doi.org/10.1615/JWomenMinorScienEng.2012002908

van den Brink M (2010) Behind the scenes of science: gender practices in the recruitment and selection of Professors in the Netherlands. Amsterdam University Press, Amsterdam

Vartan S (2019) Racial bias found in a major health care risk algorithm. Scientific American

Vikkelsø S (2007) Description as intervention: engagement and resistance in actor-network analyses. Sci Cult 16(13):297–309

Vitores A, Gil-Juárez A (2016) The trouble with "women in computing": a critical examination of the deployment of research on the gender gap in computer science. Journal of Gender Studies 25(6):666–680

Wagner I (1993) Women's voice: the case of nursing information systems. AI Soc 7(4):295–310

Wakkary R, Desjardins A, Hauser S, Maestri L (2013) A sustainable design fiction: green prac-
    tices. ACM Trans Comput Hum Interact 20(4):23
Weibert, A., A. Marshall, A. Aal, K. Schubert and J. Rode (2014). Sewing interest in E-textiles:
    analyzing making from a gendered perspective. ACM conference on designing interactive sys-
    tems, p 15–24
Winner L (1986) Do artifacts have politics? In: Winner L (ed) The whale and the reactor: a search
    for limites in an age of high technology. University of Chicaga Press, Chicago, pp 28–40
Xie B, Harpstead E, DiSalvo B, Slovak P, Kharrufa A, Lee MJ, Pammer-Schindler V, Ogan A,
    Williams JJ (2019) Learning, education, and HCI. SIG09
Zimmerman J, Forlizzi J, Evenson S (2007) Research through design as a method for interaction
    design research in HCI. Proceedings of the SIGCHI conference on human factors in computing
    systems. ACM, San Jose
Zimmerman J, Stolerman E, Forlizzi J (2010) An analysis and critique of research through design:
    towards a formalization of a research approach. DIS'10: Proceedings of the 8th ACM confer-
    ence on designing interactive systems. ACM, Aarhus
Zivony A (2019) Academia is not a meritocracy. Nat Hum Behav 3(1037)
Zuckerman H (1977) Scientific elite: nobel laureates in the United States. Transaction Publishers
Zuckerman H, Merton R (1971) Patterns of evaluation in science: institutionalisation, structure and
    functions of the referee system. Minerva 9(1):66–100
Zuiderent-Jerak T, Jensen CB (2007) Editorial introduction: unpacking 'intervention' in science
    and technology studies. Sci Cult 16(3):227–235

Printed in the United States
by Baker & Taylor Publisher Services